Delectable Fish Dishes Cookbook

Farzana P. Christie

Delectable Fish Dishes Cookbook : Mouthwatering Seafood Meals Collection: Delicious and Easy Fish Meals

Funny helpful tips:

Seek recommendations from experts in fields of interest; their insights can guide you to seminal works.

Your self-worth is not determined by societal standards; find confidence in your unique journey and abilities.

Recipes That Prove Canned Seafood Is Actually Rad As Hell

Fardeen .S Pearson

Introduction

Get ready to elevate your culinary game with this book. This comprehensive collection of recipes is your ticket to creating delectable dishes using canned crab, salmon, shrimp, and tuna. Let's dive into the tantalizing array of recipes that will delight your taste buds and impress your family and friends.

Starting with canned crab, you'll discover mouthwatering options like Best Ever Crab Cakes, Buttery Crab and Artichoke Dip, and Crab Rangoon III. From appetizers to main courses, these recipes offer a delightful fusion of flavors and textures that will leave you craving more.

Next up, canned salmon takes center stage with dishes like Asian Salmon Cakes with Creamy Miso and Sake Sauce, Easy Salmon Patties, and Salmon Chowder. Whether you're in the mood for a light salad or a hearty stew, these recipes showcase the versatility of canned salmon in creating delicious and nutritious meals.

If you're a fan of canned shrimp, you'll love recipes such as Amazing Shrimp Stuffed Mushrooms, Crab and Shrimp Pasta Salad, and Cheesy Shrimp Meltaways. These dishes are perfect for entertaining or simply enjoying a flavorful meal any day of the week.

Finally, canned tuna offers endless possibilities with recipes like Asian Spicy Tuna Salad, Best Tuna Casserole, and Creamy Tuna Noodle Casserole From Scratch. Whether you're craving a classic tuna sandwich or a comforting casserole, canned tuna is the star ingredient that brings these dishes to life.

With this book, you'll never run out of inspiration for creating delicious meals using pantry staples. Whether you're cooking for yourself or feeding a crowd, these recipes are sure to satisfy your cravings and leave you wanting more.

Contents

Chapter 1: Canned Crab Recipes

***

1. Best Ever Crab Cakes

"These are the fastest, easiest crab cakes I have ever made and some of the best I have ever eaten! Serve with coarse mustard on the plate or your favorite mustard sauce."

Serving: 4 | Prep: 15 m | Cook: 12 m | Ready in: 27 m

Ingredients

- 1 egg

- 3 tablespoons mayonnaise
- 4 teaspoons lemon juice
- 1/8 teaspoon red pepper flakes
- 1 teaspoon dried tarragon
- 1 tablespoon minced green onions
- 8 ounces crabmeat
- 1/2 cup crushed buttery round crackers
- 1 tablespoon butter

Direction

- In a medium bowl, whisk together egg, mayonnaise, lemon juice, red pepper flakes, tarragon, and scallions. Gently stir in crabmeat, being careful not to break up meat. Gradually mix in cracker crumbs, adding until desired consistency is achieved.
- Heat butter in a skillet over medium heat. Form crab mixture into 4 patties. Place patties in skillet, and cook until golden brown, about 5 to 6 minutes on each side.

Nutrition Information

- Calories: 216 calories
- Total Fat: 15.2 g
- Cholesterol: 109 mg
- Sodium: 355 mg
- Total Carbohydrate: 5.7 g
- Protein: 13.9 g

2. Buttery Crab and Artichoke Dip

"Buttery Crab and Artichoke Dip is a great, gourmet-style appetizer that is sure to turn heads at your gathering. This recipe melds our Roasted Garlic and Parmesan Baby Reds® potatoes with crab, artichoke and a variety of cheeses."

Serving: 8

Ingredients

- 1 (4.1 ounce) package Idahoan® Roasted Garlic Parmesan Baby Reds
- 2 (6 ounce) cans lump crabmeat, drained
- 2 (15 ounce) cans water packed artichoke hearts
- 1 cup Brie cheese, broken into chunks
- 1 cup shredded Gruyere cheese
- 1/2 cup shredded Parmesan cheese
- 1 cup boiling water

Direction

- Preheat oven to 400 degrees F.
- Add all ingredients in a large mixing bowl and fold carefully. Use the water from the canned artichokes along with the boiling water.
- Place in a 9 x 12 baking dish that has been sprayed with olive oil.
- Bake until bubbling and golden brown.
- Serve with baguettes or crackers.

Nutrition Information

- Calories: 250 calories
- Total Fat: 11.5 g
- Cholesterol: 74 mg
- Sodium: 1107 mg
- Total Carbohydrate: 14.6 g
- Protein: 22.5 g

3. Cajun Crab Rangoon

"This is a great Cajun take on an Asian appetizer."

Serving: 60 | Prep: 30 m | Cook: 20 m | Ready in: 50 m

Ingredients

- 6 slices bacon, chopped
- 1/2 onion, minced
- 2 (8 ounce) packages cream cheese, softened
- 2 tablespoons hot pepper sauce (such as Tabasco®)
- 2 tablespoons Worcestershire sauce
- 3 tablespoons chopped fresh dill
- 1 cup cooked and peeled crawfish tails, coarsely chopped
- 1 cup lump crabmeat, picked over
- salt and black pepper to taste
- 1 (16 ounce) package wonton wrappers
- 1 egg, beaten
- 2 cups vegetable oil for frying

Direction

- Cook the bacon in a saucepan over medium heat until the bacon is limp, and is beginning to release its grease, about 3 minutes. Stir in the onion, and cook until the onion has softened and turned translucent, about 5 minutes. Scrape the onion mixture into a mixing bowl, and stir in the cream cheese, hot pepper sauce, Worcestershire sauce, dill, and crawfish tails. Gently fold in the crabmeat, then season to taste with salt and pepper.

- To make the wontons: Separate and place the wonton wrappers onto your work surface. Spoon about 1 tablespoon of the seafood filling onto the center of each wrapper. Use your finger or a pastry brush to lightly moisten the edges of the wonton wrappers with the beaten egg. Fold each corner of the wrapper over the filling, and press together over the center of the won ton. Press the edges together to seal.
- Heat oil in a deep-fryer or large saucepan to 350 degrees F (175 degrees C).
- Fry the won tons in the hot oil until they turn golden brown and float, about 2 minutes. Drain on a paper towel-lined plate before serving.

Nutrition Information

- Calories: 75 calories
- Total Fat: 4.9 g
- Cholesterol: 20 mg
- Sodium: 109 mg
- Total Carbohydrate: 4.9 g
- Protein: 2.8 g

4. **Chrissys Tangy Seafood Dip**

"I love the Olive Garden's San Remo seafood dip and this is my attempt at trying to copy it. It is very popular at family gatherings!"

Serving: 8 | Prep: 10 m | Cook: 40 m | Ready in: 50 m

Ingredients

- 1 cup meatless spaghetti sauce
- 1 (6 ounce) can crabmeat, drained and flaked
- 1 (8 ounce) package cream cheese, softened
- 1 cup shredded white Cheddar cheese
- 2 tablespoons OLD BAY® Seasoning
- 2 tablespoons Worcestershire sauce
- 1 teaspoon ground black pepper
- 1/2 teaspoon kosher salt

Direction

- Preheat the oven to 350 degrees F (175 degrees C).
- Spread the spaghetti sauce in an even layer in the bottom of an 8 or 9 inch square baking dish. In a medium bowl, mix together the crabmeat, cream cheese, and Cheddar cheese. Season with Old Bay, Worcestershire sauce, pepper, and salt. Spoon over the spaghetti sauce layer, and spread evenly.
- Bake for 40 minutes in the preheated oven, or until the top is golden brown. Serve immediately with thinly sliced baguettes or crackers.

Nutrition Information

- Calories: 210 calories
- Total Fat: 15.7 g
- Cholesterol: 65 mg
- Sodium: 939 mg
- Total Carbohydrate: 6.7 g
- Protein: 10.7 g

5. Crab and Corn Cakes with Roasted PepperYogurt Aioli

"Whole wheat panko crumbs and cornmeal add a golden crunch to these sweet corn and crabmeat appetizer cakes. The tangy Greek yogurt-red pepper aioli topper adds a creamy contrast to the summery dish."

Serving: 6 | Prep: 30 m | Cook: 12 m | Ready in: 42 m

Ingredients

- 1/2 cup whole wheat panko bread crumbs
- 1/2 cup cornmeal
- 1/4 teaspoon salt
- 1/4 teaspoon black pepper
- 1 (5.3 ounce) container VOSKOS® Nonfat Vanilla Greek Yogurt
- 3 eggs, lightly beaten
- 2 cups fresh or frozen corn kernels (thawed, if frozen)
- 1 (6 ounce) can crabmeat, drained, flaked and cartilage removed
- 2 tablespoons olive oil
- Roasted Pepper-Yogurt Aioli:
- 2 (5.3 ounce) containers VOSKOS® Nonfat Vanilla Greek Yogurt
- 1/4 cup roasted red peppers, drained
- 4 teaspoons lemon juice
- 2 cloves garlic, minced

Direction

- Stir together the whole wheat panko, cornmeal, salt, and pepper. Whisk in VOSKOS(R) Nonfat Vanilla Greek Yogurt and eggs until combined. Stir in corn and crabmeat.

- Coat a very large nonstick skillet with olive oil. Heat over medium-high heat. Using a 1/4-cup measure, add six portions of the corn-crab mixture to the hot skillet, spacing evenly. Cook about 6 minutes or until golden brown, turning once. Transfer to a warm serving plate. Repeat with remaining corn-crab mixture. Serve warm with Roasted Pepper-Yogurt Aioli (see below).
- Roasted Pepper-Yogurt Aioli: Add VOSKOS(R) Nonfat Vanilla Greek Yogurt, red pepper, lemon juice, and garlic to a blender or food processor. Cover and blend until smooth.

Nutrition Information

- Calories: 271 calories
- Total Fat: 8.3 g
- Cholesterol: 108 mg
- Sodium: 281 mg
- Total Carbohydrate: 35.1 g
- Protein: 16.4 g

6. Crab and Lobster Stuffed Mushrooms

"This is the result of trying to duplicate a seafood chain's recipe. Comes close enough, they're gone the minute they hit the table!"

Serving: 8 | Prep: 10 m | Cook: 10 m | Ready in: 20 m

Ingredients

- 3/4 cup melted butter, divided
- 1 pound fresh mushrooms, stems removed
- 1 cup crushed seasoned croutons
- 1 cup shredded mozzarella cheese
- 1 (6 ounce) can crabmeat, drained
- 1 pound lobster tail, cleaned and chopped
- 3 tablespoons minced garlic
- 1/4 cup shredded mozzarella cheese (optional)

Direction

- Preheat the oven to 375 degrees F (190 degrees C). Brush a large baking sheet with about 1/4 cup of melted butter. Arrange mushroom caps in a single layer over the baking sheet.
- In a medium bowl, mix together the crushed croutons, remaining 1/2 cup butter, shredded cheese, crabmeat, lobster and garlic. Spoon into mushroom caps where the stems used to be.
- Bake for 10 to 12 minutes in the preheated oven, or until lightly browned on the top. Sprinkle with additional cheese if desired, and serve hot!

Nutrition Information

- Calories: 310 calories
- Total Fat: 22 g
- Cholesterol: 130 mg
- Sodium: 535 mg
- Total Carbohydrate: 6.9 g
- Protein: 21.9 g

7. **Crab and Red Pepper Soup**

"A lighter version of your favorite seafood bisque. Adjust the ingredient amounts for flavor or thickness preference! It is delicious served alongside steamed broccoli and a piece of crusty bread!"

Serving: 2 | Prep: 25 m | Cook: 35 m | Ready in: 1 h

Ingredients

- 1 red bell pepper, seeded and quartered
- 1 teaspoon olive oil
- 1 large stalk celery, diced
- 1 clove garlic, diced
- 1/2 small sweet onion, chopped
- 1 (6 ounce) can white crabmeat, drained, flaked
- 1/2 teaspoon dried rosemary
- 1/8 teaspoon lemon-pepper seasoning
- 1 cup chicken stock
- 1/2 cup dry potato flakes
- 1/4 cup fat-free milk
- 2 tablespoons sour cream
- 2 tablespoons grated Asiago cheese, for garnish (optional)

Direction

- Preheat the oven's broiler, and set the oven rack at about 6 inches from the heat source. Line a baking sheet with aluminum foil. Place the peppers, cut sides down, onto the prepared baking sheet.
- Cook under the preheated broiler until the skin of the peppers has blackened and blistered, about 5 minutes. Place the

blackened peppers into a bowl, and tightly seal with plastic wrap. Allow the peppers to steam as they cool, about 20 minutes. Once cool, remove the skins and dice. Set aside.

- Heat the olive oil in a large saucepan over medium heat. Stir in the celery, garlic, and onion; cook and stir until the onion has softened and turned translucent, about 5 minutes. Stir in the roasted red bell pepper and crabmeat, and season with rosemary and lemon pepper. Pour in the chicken stock, and simmer for 10 minutes. Slowly stir in the dry potato flakes, and cook until thickened.
- Pour the soup into a blender, filling the pitcher no more than halfway full. Hold down the lid of the blender with a folded kitchen towel, and carefully start the blender, using a few quick pulses to get the soup moving before leaving it on to puree. Puree in batches until smooth and pour into a clean pot. Alternately, you can use a stick blender and puree the soup right in the cooking pot.
- Return the pureed soup to the saucepan. Stir in the milk and sour cream, and cook over medium-low heat until heated through, about 5 minutes. Top with Asiago cheese before serving.

Nutrition Information

- Calories: 251 calories
- Total Fat: 9 g
- Cholesterol: 88 mg
- Sodium: 795 mg
- Total Carbohydrate: 19.3 g
- Protein: 22.8 g

8. Crab and Salmon Dip

"This is always a smash hit at my casual dinner parties. Arrange crackers around dip for easy serving."

Serving: 24 | Prep: 15 m | Cook: 5 m | Ready in: 20 m

Ingredients

- 2 tablespoons butter
- 1 small onion, finely chopped
- 1 (8 ounce) package cream cheese, softened
- 1 cup plain yogurt
- 2 (6 ounce) cans lump crabmeat, drained
- 6 ounces smoked salmon, chopped
- 1/4 teaspoon garlic salt
- 1 pinch ground black pepper
- 1 tablespoon chopped Italian flat leaf parsley

Direction

- Melt butter in small skillet over medium heat. Add onion; cook and stir until onion is translucent, about 5 minutes. Set aside to cool.
- Stir together cream cheese, yogurt, crab meat, and salmon in a bowl. Stir in cooled onion. Season with garlic salt and black pepper. Pour mixture into a shallow serving bowl and sprinkle with parsley.

Nutrition Information

- Calories: 71 calories

- Total Fat: 4.9 g
- Cholesterol: 28 mg
- Sodium: 163 mg
- Total Carbohydrate: 1.3 g
- Protein: 5.5 g

9. Crab and Seafood Stuffed Shells

"These shells stuffed with a creamy seafood mixture will delight your guests."

Serving: 6 | Prep: 20 m | Cook: 15 m | Ready in: 35 m

Ingredients

- 1 (12 ounce) box jumbo pasta shells
- 1 (6 ounce) can crabmeat, drained
- 1 (6.5 ounce) can small shrimp, drained
- 3 teaspoons minced celery
- 1 tablespoon minced onion
- 1 cup creamy salad dressing (such as Miracle Whip®)
- 1 cup shredded Swiss cheese

Direction

- Fill a large pot with lightly salted water and bring to a rolling boil over high heat. Once the water is boiling, stir in the pasta shells, and return to a boil. Cook uncovered, stirring occasionally, until the pasta has cooked through, but is still firm to the bite, about 13 minutes. well in a colander set in the sink, then rinse with cold water until the pasta is cold. Drain thoroughly.
- While the pasta is cooking, stir the crabmeat, shrimp, celery, onion, and creamy salad dressing in a mixing bowl. Stir in the shredded Swiss cheese.
- Stuff each shell with some of the seafood mixture, and place into a serving dish. Keep refrigerated until ready to serve.

Nutrition Information

- Calories: 450 calories
- Total Fat: 17.3 g
- Cholesterol: 92 mg
- Sodium: 501 mg
- Total Carbohydrate: 48.5 g
- Protein: 22.8 g

10. Crab Cakes Chiarello

"These chunky crab cakes with fresh herbs, mustard, lemon and mayo are coated with seasoned panko bread crumbs, and baked until golden brown."

Serving: 18 | Prep: 35 m | Ready in: 1 h 5 m

Ingredients

- 1 1/2 cups Progresso® panko crispy bread crumbs
- 1 cup mayonnaise or salad dressing
- 2 tablespoons chopped fresh parsley
- 1 tablespoon finely chopped chives
- 1 tablespoon lemon juice
- 2 teaspoons Dijon mustard
- 1/8 teaspoon freshly ground pepper
- 2 drops red pepper sauce
- 2 egg yolks
- 3 (6 ounce) cans lump crabmeat, well drained
- 1 cup Progresso® panko crispy bread crumbs
- 2 tablespoons butter, melted
- 1 1/2 teaspoons seafood seasoning

Direction

- Heat oven to 425 degrees F. In medium bowl, mix 1 1/2 cups bread crumbs, the mayonnaise, parsley, chives, lemon juice, mustard, pepper, pepper sauce and egg yolks. Using rubber spatula, gently fold in crabmeat, keeping pieces as large as possible.
- Shape mixture by 1/4 cupfuls into 18 patties, 2 1/2 inches in diameter.

- In medium bowl, mix remaining ingredients. Dip crab cakes into crumb mixture, coating both sides. Place in 2 ungreased 15x10-inch pans with sides.
- Bake both pans on separate oven racks 12 to 15 minutes, turning patties once after 6 minutes, until golden brown. Serve warm.

Nutrition Information

- Calories: 269 calories
- Total Fat: 16.9 g
- Cholesterol: 56 mg
- Sodium: 715 mg
- Total Carbohydrate: 21 g
- Protein: 8.4 g

11. Crab Cakes with Remoulade Sauce

"The best crab cakes are freshly made and cooked in your skillet just until crunchy on the outside. The remoulade sauce is inspired by New Orleans cooking, and you can adjust the spice levels with more or less horseradish and Louisiana-style hot sauce. Crisp French fries make a great side, but you can go lighter with marinated green bean salad."

Serving: 6 | Prep: 30 m | Cook: 10 m | Ready in: 40 m

Ingredients

- 8 Ball Park® Hamburger Buns
- 1 tablespoon butter, melted, or more as needed
- Remoulade Sauce:
- 3/4 cup mayonnaise
- 3 tablespoons chopped green onion
- 1 tablespoon grainy mustard
- 1 tablespoon chopped fresh flat-leaf parsley
- 2 teaspoons ketchup
- 2 teaspoons white wine vinegar
- 1 teaspoon prepared horseradish
- 1 teaspoon garlic granules
- 2 dashes hot pepper sauce (such as Tabasco®), or to taste
- salt and pepper to taste
- Crab Cakes:
- 1/4 cup mayonnaise
- 1 large egg, beaten
- 1 1/2 teaspoons minced red onion
- 1/2 tablespoon minced Italian parsley
- 2 (6 ounce) cans crabmeat, drained, picked clean

- 2 cups fine bread or cracker crumbs, divided
- 3 teaspoons seafood seasoning (such as Old Bay®)
- 1/2 teaspoon sea salt
- 2 tablespoons ground black pepper
- 1 pinch cayenne pepper
- 2 tablespoons vegetable oil
- Trimmings to include lettuce, tomato and onion, as desired, plus lemon wedges

Direction

- To make sauce, combine all ingredients in a medium bowl and whisk well. Cover and hold in refrigerator.
- To make crab cakes, combine mayonnaise, egg, red onion and parsley in a large bowl, stirring well with a fork.
- Add crab, 1 cup bread crumbs, seafood seasoning, salt, pepper, paprika and cayenne. Stir until combined; the mixture will be fairly loose and wet.
- Shape mixture into 8 patties of equal size. Coat each patty in remaining bread crumbs to make a crust.
- In a large skillet, heat oil over medium heat and cook patties for about 8 minutes, turning just once about halfway through cooking, just until uniformly golden brown.
- Meanwhile, brush hamburger buns with melted butter and toast at 400 degrees F just until they begin to brown at edges.
- To serve, place patty on each bun, top with remoulade sauce and desired trimmings. Serve with extra sauce and lemon wedges on the table.

Nutrition Information

- Calories: 707 calories

- Total Fat: 41.2 g
- Cholesterol: 100 mg
- Sodium: 1441 mg
- Total Carbohydrate: 62.7 g
- Protein: 25.1 g

12. Crab Casserole

"This casserole is easy and yummy. You can substitute tuna or salmon if you like."

Serving: 6 | Prep: 15 m | Cook: 30 m | Ready in: 45 m

Ingredients

- 1 (14.5 ounce) can green beans
- 2 (6 ounce) cans crabmeat
- 3 teaspoons all-purpose flour, divided
- 1 (8 ounce) package Cheddar cheese, shredded
- 1 (6 ounce) can French-fried onion rings
- 1 (10.25 ounce) can condensed tomato soup
- 1 (10.75 ounce) can milk
- 1 (10 ounce) can refrigerated biscuit dough

Direction

- Preheat oven to 350 degrees F (175 degrees C).
- In a 2 quart casserole layer the beans, crab, 1 teaspoon flour, cheese and all but 1/3 cup onion rings.
- In a small bowl mix together the soup and milk; stir in remaining 2 teaspoons flour and pour mixture over casserole.
- Bake in the preheated oven for 10 minutes or until bubbly. Arrange biscuits on top of casserole and bake for another 20 minutes, adding remaining onion rings in the last 3 minutes of baking.

Nutrition Information

- Calories: 612 calories
- Total Fat: 34.4 g
- Cholesterol: 94 mg
- Sodium: 1611 mg
- Total Carbohydrate: 46 g
- Protein: 27 g

13. Crab Dip I

"Everyone will love the flavor of crabmeat in this creamy dip that is simple to prepare and delicious when served with chips or crackers. Adjust the amount of celery to taste."

Serving: 12 | Prep: 10 m | Ready in: 1 h 10 m

Ingredients

- 1 onion
- 1/2 cup creamy salad dressing
- 1 (3 ounce) package cream cheese, softened
- 1/2 cup crabmeat
- 1/2 teaspoon lemon juice
- 1/2 teaspoon Worcestershire sauce
- 1 stalk chopped celery

Direction

- Extract and reserve 1/2 teaspoon juice from the onion.
- In a mixing bowl, combine the onion juice, creamy salad dressing, cream cheese, crabmeat, lemon juice, Worcestershire sauce and celery. Thoroughly blend all the ingredients until they are smooth and creamy. Allow the dip to chill in the refrigerator for at least 1 hour.

Nutrition Information

- Calories: 65 calories
- Total Fat: 5.2 g
- Cholesterol: 16 mg

- Sodium: 128 mg
- Total Carbohydrate: 2.5 g
- Protein: 1.8 g

14. Crab Imperial I

"This is a recipe that I devised many years ago using several different recipes. It can be served as a main meal or used to stuff mushrooms as an appetizer"

Serving: 4 | Prep: 10 m | Cook: 25 m | Ready in: 35 m

Ingredients

- 1 pound crabmeat
- 1 green bell pepper, chopped
- 1 tablespoon chopped pimento peppers
- 3 tablespoons mayonnaise
- 1 egg
- 1 tablespoon Worcestershire sauce
- 1 teaspoon salt
- 1/4 teaspoon mustard powder
- 1 dash hot pepper sauce

Direction

- Preheat oven to 350 degrees F (175 degrees C).
- In a medium bowl, combine the crabmeat, bell pepper, pimento, mayonnaise, egg, Worcestershire sauce, salt, mustard powder and red pepper sauce. Mix well and spoon into a shallow 1 1/2-quart baking dish.
- Bake at 350 degrees F (175 degrees C) for 20 to 25 minutes.

Nutrition Information

- Calories: 216 calories
- Total Fat: 11 g

- Cholesterol: 151 mg
- Sodium: 1085 mg
- Total Carbohydrate: 2.9 g
- Protein: 25.3 g

15. Crab N Shrimp Dip

"I always have this for a filler with company around the holidays, fun to serve with holiday shaped crackers that are available."

Serving: 18

Ingredients

- 8 ounces cream cheese, softened
- 1 tablespoon mayonnaise
- 1 green onion, chopped
- 1 (6 ounce) can crab meat, drained
- 1 (4.5 ounce) can small shrimp, drained

Direction

- Blend together the cream cheese and mayonnaise. Add the green onion, crab and shrimp. Place in a covered container and chill overnight.

Nutrition Information

- Calories: 68 calories
- Total Fat: 5.3 g
- Cholesterol: 35 mg
- Sodium: 85 mg
- Total Carbohydrate: 0.5 g
- Protein: 4.5 g

16. Crab Rangoon I

"Everyone will love these bite-size, fried dumplings stuffed with crab. You can make these in advance of the festivities, and freeze on trays until party time."

Serving: 10 | Prep: 20 m | Cook: 10 m | Ready in: 30 m

Ingredients

- 1 (14 ounce) package small won ton wrappers
- 2 (8 ounce) packages cream cheese, softened
- 1 teaspoon minced fresh ginger root
- 1/2 teaspoon chopped fresh cilantro
- 1/2 teaspoon dried parsley
- 3 tablespoons dark soy sauce
- 1 pound crabmeat, shredded
- 1 quart oil for frying

Direction

- Heat oil in a large heavy skillet or deep fryer to 360 degrees F (180 degrees C).
- In a small bowl, mix together cream cheese, soy sauce, ginger, garlic, parsley, cilantro and crabmeat.
- Place 1/2 to 1 teaspoon of the cream cheese mixture into the center of each wonton wrapper. Fold the won ton wrapper over the stuffing to make a triangle or a half moon, depending on the shape of the won ton wrappers you have purchased. Moisten the edges with a little water, and seal. Place prepared won tons under a slightly moist paper towel until ready for frying.
- Add 3 or 4 wontons to the hot oil, and cook until golden brown, turning once. Set aside on paper towels to drain. Repeat until

all wontons have been fried. Serve hot.

Nutrition Information

- Calories: 393 calories
- Total Fat: 25.6 g
- Cholesterol: 93 mg
- Sodium: 778 mg
- Total Carbohydrate: 23.9 g
- Protein: 16.5 g

17. Crab Rangoon III

"Crabmeat and cream cheese wontons make excellent appetizers. Leave out the water chestnuts, if desired. Serve with your favorite Asian-style dipping sauces."

Serving: 15 | Prep: 25 m | Cook: 20 m | Ready in: 45 m

Ingredients

- 1 quart oil for deep frying
- 1 (8 ounce) package cream cheese, softened
- 2 (6 ounce) cans crabmeat, drained and flaked
- 1/2 teaspoon garlic powder
- 1/4 teaspoon paprika
- 2 tablespoons water chestnuts, drained and chopped
- 1 (14 ounce) package wonton wrappers

Direction

- In a large, heavy sauce pan heat oil to 375 degrees F (190 degrees C).
- In a medium bowl, mix cream cheese, crabmeat, garlic powder, paprika and water chestnuts.
- Place approximately 1 teaspoon of the cream cheese mixture in the center of wonton wrappers. Moisten wrapper edges with water, fold over the mixture and pinch to seal.
- In small batches, fry the wontons 3 to 5 minutes, or until golden brown.

Nutrition Information

- Calories: 203 calories

- Total Fat: 11.7 g
- Cholesterol: 39 mg
- Sodium: 268 mg
- Total Carbohydrate: 15.8 g
- Protein: 8.3 g

18. Crab Spread I

"An easy, but filling appetizer for your next party. Serve with small serving knife over assorted crackers."

Serving: 4 | Prep: 5 m | Ready in: 5 m

Ingredients

- 1 (8 ounce) package cream cheese, softened
- 1 (6 ounce) can crab meat, drained
- 1 (12 ounce) jar cocktail sauce
- 1 lemon, juiced

Direction

- Place cream cheese on large plate. Cover with crabmeat, squeeze juice of one lemon over the crabmeat. Pour cocktail sauce over top of the entire concoction.

Nutrition Information

- Calories: 319 calories
- Total Fat: 20.8 g
- Cholesterol: 99 mg
- Sodium: 1325 mg
- Total Carbohydrate: 20.9 g
- Protein: 14.4 g

19. Crab Stuffed Manicotti

"Manicotti shells stuffed with crab meat and covered with Alfredo sauce make a great meal for family or company."

Serving: 4 | Prep: 20 m | Cook: 35 m | Ready in: 55 m

Ingredients

- 8 manicotti shells
- 1 1/2 cups ricotta cheese
- 1 (6 ounce) can lump crabmeat
- 2 tablespoons minced fresh parsley
- 1 tablespoon grated onion
- 1 (16 ounce) jar Alfredo pasta sauce
- 1 teaspoon white sugar
- 1/2 cup chicken broth
- 1/2 teaspoon dried basil
- 1/2 teaspoon dried marjoram
- 1/8 teaspoon garlic powder
- 1/8 teaspoon dried thyme

Direction

- Preheat the oven to 375 degrees F (190 degrees C).
- Bring a large pot of lightly salted water to a boil. Add manicotti shells and cook for 8 to 10 minutes, until tender but not mushy. Drain.
- In a medium bowl, stir together the ricotta cheese, crab, parsley and onion. Spoon into the manicotti shells. Place in a buttered 11x7 inch baking dish.

- In a saucepan, stir together the Alfredo sauce and chicken broth. Season with basil, marjoram, garlic powder and thyme. Heat until warm over medium heat. Pour over the shells in the baking dish.
- Bake uncovered for 30 minutes in the preheated oven. Let stand for about 5 minutes before serving.

Nutrition Information

- Calories: 498 calories
- Total Fat: 34.3 g
- Cholesterol: 83 mg
- Sodium: 1242 mg
- Total Carbohydrate: 31.4 g
- Protein: 18.7 g

20. Crab Swiss Bites

"These hot appetizer bites are delicious and easy to make. Rolls are separated into pieces, topped with a crabmeat and Swiss cheese mixture, and sprinkled with water chestnuts. They're a definite crowd pleaser!"

Serving: 10 | Prep: 10 m | Cook: 12 m | Ready in: 22 m

Ingredients

- 1 (6 ounce) can crabmeat, drained and flaked
- 1 tablespoon sliced green onion
- 1/4 cup shredded Swiss cheese
- 1/2 cup mayonnaise
- 1 teaspoon lemon juice
- 1/4 teaspoon curry powder
- 1 (8 ounce) package dinner rolls
- 1 (5 ounce) can water chestnuts, drained and sliced

Direction

- Preheat oven to 400 degrees F (200 degrees C).
- In a medium bowl, mix together crabmeat, green onion, Swiss cheese, mayonnaise, lemon juice and curry powder.
- Separate dinner rolls into 3 pieces each. Spoon equal portions of the crabmeat mixture onto the roll pieces. Top with water chestnuts.
- Bake in the preheated oven 10 to 12 minutes, or until bubbly and golden brown.

Nutrition Information

- Calories: 114 calories
- Total Fat: 9.7 g
- Cholesterol: 22 mg
- Sodium: 125 mg
- Total Carbohydrate: 2.4 g
- Protein: 4.4 g

21. Crab Tuna Souffle

"My dad used to make this recipe when I was a child. It was the only way I would eat seafood. Now that I've become a seafood lover, I really enjoy this one even more! Good for special occasions since it has to be chilled overnight."

Serving: 8 | Prep: 20 m | Cook: 1 h 15 m | Ready in: 4 h 35 m

Ingredients

- 1 (6 ounce) can crabmeat, drained and flaked
- 1 (5 ounce) can tuna, drained and flaked
- 4 cups cubed French bread
- 8 ounces Muenster cheese, cubed
- 2 tablespoons chopped fresh parsley
- 4 eggs
- 3 cups milk
- 3 tablespoons butter
- 2 teaspoons mustard powder
- 1 teaspoon grated onion

Direction

- In a small bowl, stir together the crabmeat and tuna. Place a layer of bread cubes in the bottom of a 1 1/2 quart casserole dish. Cover with a layer of the crab and tuna, then a layer of cheese and a sprinkle of parsley. Repeat layers 2 more times ending with cheese and parsley on top.
- In a medium bowl, whisk together the eggs, milk, butter, mustard powder and onion. Pour over the layers in the dish. Cover and refrigerate for at least 3 hours, or overnight.

- Preheat the oven to 350 degrees F (175 degrees C). Let the dish come to room temperature while the oven preheats.
- Bake uncovered for 1 hour and 15 minutes in the preheated oven, or until puffed and golden.

Nutrition Information

- Calories: 419 calories
- Total Fat: 18.8 g
- Cholesterol: 162 mg
- Sodium: 701 mg
- Total Carbohydrate: 34.7 g
- Protein: 27.6 g

22. Crab Wonton Cups

"This appetizer has an unusual combination of ingredients, but they are easy to make and delicious. I am always asked for the recipe whenever I serve them. May be frozen and reheated."

Serving: 24 | Prep: 20 m | Cook: 12 m | Ready in: 32 m

Ingredients

- 1 (6 ounce) can crabmeat, drained
- 1 tablespoon chopped green onions
- 1/2 cup mayonnaise
- 1/2 teaspoon curry powder
- 1/2 teaspoon salt
- 1 teaspoon lemon juice
- 1 cup shredded Swiss cheese
- 1 (8 ounce) can sliced water chestnuts, drained
- 24 wonton wrappers

Direction

- Preheat oven to 400 degrees F (200 degrees C). Spray mini-muffin tins with nonstick cooking spray.
- In a medium bowl, stir together crabmeat, green onion, mayonnaise, curry powder, salt, lemon juice, and Swiss cheese. Use kitchen scissors to trim off corners of individual wonton skins; place trimmed skins in wells of mini-muffin tins. Spoon about 1 tablespoon crabmeat mixture into each wonton cup. Top each with a slice of water chestnut.
- Bake in preheated oven about 12 minutes, or until puffed and browned. Serve hot.

Nutrition Information

- Calories: 107 calories
- Total Fat: 6.7 g
- Cholesterol: 18 mg
- Sodium: 164 mg
- Total Carbohydrate: 6.5 g
- Protein: 5.1 g

23. CrabArtichoke Pizza

"I used leftover crabmeat and artichokes from another meal, and this turned out delicious! Enjoy! Fresh pizza dough can often be found in the deli section of supermarkets."

Serving: 4 | Prep: 15 m | Cook: 25 m | Ready in: 40 m

Ingredients

- 1 pound fresh pizza dough
- 1/4 teaspoon red pepper flakes
- 1 (6 ounce) can crabmeat - drained and cartilage removed
- 1 (6 ounce) jar quartered artichoke hearts in water, drained
- 2 tablespoons olive oil
- 1 1/2 tablespoons minced garlic
- 1/2 cup shredded Parmesan cheese
- 1 cup shredded mozzarella cheese

Direction

- Preheat oven to 350 degrees F (175 degrees C). Lightly grease a pizza pan.
- Roll out pizza dough on a floured surface to a 14 or 16 inch circle; place onto a pizza pan. Sprinkle dough with red pepper flakes, then top evenly with crab and artichokes. Drizzle with olive oil, then sprinkle with garlic, Parmesan cheese, and mozzarella cheese.
- Bake in preheated oven until the cheese has melted and the crust is no longer doughy, about 20 minutes. Set oven to broil, and cook pizza for 5 minutes more until the cheese has begun to brown.

Nutrition Information

- Calories: 541 calories
- Total Fat: 18.5 g
- Cholesterol: 63 mg
- Sodium: 1497 mg
- Total Carbohydrate: 60.5 g
- Protein: 30.9 g

24. Crabby Cliffs Mushroom Puffs

"These crab and mushroom filled pastry puff squares have become a family favorite! We enjoy them as finger food on Saturday nights while watching a hockey game or entertaining guests."

Serving: 18 | Prep: 20 m | Cook: 20 m | Ready in: 40 m

Ingredients

- 2 tablespoons olive oil
- 3 cups fresh chopped mushrooms
- 2 green onions, chopped
- 1 clove garlic, crushed
- 1/2 teaspoon ground cayenne pepper
- 4 ounces cream cheese, softened
- 1 (6 ounce) can crabmeat, drained and flaked
- 1 (17.5 ounce) package frozen puff pastry sheets, thawed

Direction

- Preheat oven to 400 degrees F (200 degrees C).
- Heat the olive oil in a medium saucepan over medium heat. Stir in the mushrooms, green onions, garlic and cayenne pepper. Cook 10 minutes, or until tender. Transfer the mushroom mixture to a medium bowl. Blend in the cream cheese and crabmeat.
- On a lightly floured flat surface, roll each pastry sheet into a 12x12 inch square. Cut each sheet into nine 4x4 inch squares. Place 1 tablespoon of the mushroom mixture onto each pastry square. Fold the squares by bringing the corners to the center, creating an X. Place the squares on a medium baking sheet.

- Bake 20 minutes in the preheated oven, or until golden brown.

Nutrition Information

- Calories: 199 calories
- Total Fat: 14.3 g
- Cholesterol: 15 mg
- Sodium: 119 mg
- Total Carbohydrate: 13.2 g
- Protein: 4.9 g

25. Crabby Crusted Chickpea Cakes

"Crab salad tops a garbanzo bean-based patty with an oatmeal crust, all stacked on top of shredded lettuce."

Serving: 10 | Prep: 45 m | Cook: 6 m | Ready in: 51 m

Ingredients

- 2 (15 ounce) cans chickpeas (garbanzo beans), drained and rinsed
- 1 onion, chopped
- 1/2 cup chopped fresh parsley, divided
- 2 eggs, beaten
- 1 teaspoon salt
- 1/2 teaspoon ground black pepper
- 1/4 teaspoon dried thyme
- 1 1/2 cups quick-cooking oats, divided
- 3/4 cup bread crumbs, divided
- 1/4 cup grapeseed oil
- 2 (6 ounce) cans crab meat, drained
- 1/4 cup mayonnaise
- 1 tablespoon celery seed
- 1 1/2 teaspoons white sugar
- 1/2 teaspoon paprika
- 1 large head romaine lettuce heart, shredded

Direction

- Blend chickpeas together in a food processor or blender until they turn into a paste; transfer to a bowl. Mix onion, 1/4 cup parsley, eggs, salt, black pepper, and thyme into chickpeas paste. Add 1/2 of the oats and 1/2 of the bread crumbs.
- Spread the remaining oats and bread crumbs onto a plate.
- Form chickpea mixture into patties; press into oat-bread crumb mixture into completely coated.
- Heat oil in a large skillet over medium heat; add patties and cook until patties are golden brown, 3 to 4 minutes per side.
- Mix crab meat, mayonnaise, celery seed, sugar, and paprika together in a bowl until crab salad is well mixed.
- Place a bed of lettuce on a serving plate; top with chickpea patties. Spoon crab salad on top of each patty.

Nutrition Information

- Calories: 302 calories
- Total Fat: 13.4 g
- Cholesterol: 69 mg
- Sodium: 624 mg
- Total Carbohydrate: 31.5 g
- Protein: 14.6 g

26. Crabmeat Bake Special

"Delicious for lunch or a light dinner."

Serving: 6 | Prep: 10 m | Cook: 25 m | Ready in: 35 m

Ingredients

- 1 (6 ounce) can canned crabmeat, drained
- 1 cup fresh bread crumbs
- 1 cup mayonnaise
- 3/4 cup milk
- 6 hard-cooked eggs, chopped
- 1/3 cup onion, diced
- 1 teaspoon salt

Direction

- Preheat oven to 350 degrees F (175 degrees C).
- Place eggs in a saucepan and cover with cold water. Bring water to a boil and immediately remove from heat. Cover and let eggs stand in hot water for 10 to 12 minutes. Remove from hot water, cool, peel and chop.
- In a mixing bowl, combine the crab, bread crumbs, mayonnaise, milk, chopped eggs, onion, and salt. Mix thoroughly. Pour into a 1 quart casserole dish.
- Bake in a preheated oven for 25 minutes or until the top is lightly brown and bubbly.

Nutrition Information

- Calories: 459 calories
- Total Fat: 36.3 g
- Cholesterol: 253 mg
- Sodium: 896 mg
- Total Carbohydrate: 17 g
- Protein: 15.9 g

27. Crabmeat Canapes

"Easy and wonderful crab canapes made on English muffins. They can be made and frozen ahead of time. Cooked pork sausage may be substituted for crabmeat."

Serving: 25 | Prep: 5 m | Cook: 12 m | Ready in: 17 m

Ingredients

- 1/2 cup butter, softened
- 1 cup processed cheese sauce
- 1/2 teaspoon garlic salt
- 1/2 teaspoon seasoning salt
- 1 (6 ounce) can crabmeat
- 6 English muffins, split in half

Direction

- In a medium mixing bowl, blend butter, cheese, garlic salt, seasoning salt, and crab meat. Spread mixture on split muffins. Freeze until ready to use. When ready, thaw for 10 minutes.
- Preheat oven to 400 degrees F (200 degrees C).
- Cut muffins into 6 pie shaped slices and place on cookie sheet.
- Bake at 400 degrees F (200 degrees C) for 12 minutes.

Nutrition Information

- Calories: 99 calories
- Total Fat: 6.2 g
- Cholesterol: 24 mg
- Sodium: 333 mg

- Total Carbohydrate: 7 g
- Protein: 3.9 g

28. Creole Crab Noodles

"Crab, and its old friends, the Holy Trinity, are a classic combo, and so it was no surprise they worked so well in an Asian-style rice noodle dish ◆an experiment gone right. Garnish with sliced green onion."

Serving: 2 | Prep: 20 m | Cook: 15 m | Ready in: 35 m

Ingredients

- For the Sauce:
- 3 cloves garlic, crushed
- 3 tablespoons ketchup
- 1/4 cup seasoned rice vinegar
- 1 tablespoon soy sauce
- 1 tablespoon fish sauce (optional)
- 1 tablespoon hot sauce, or to taste
- 1 teaspoon paprika
- 1/2 teaspoon cayenne pepper
- 1 teaspoon ground cumin
- 8 ounces rice noodles
- 2 tablespoons vegetable oil
- 1/3 cup diced celery
- 1/3 cup minced red and green jalapenos
- 1/3 cup diced green onions
- 1/2 pound crabmeat

Direction

- Whisk garlic, ketchup, rice vinegar, soy sauce, fish sauce, hot sauce, paprika, cayenne pepper, and cumin together in a bowl.

- Place rice noodles in a large bowl; cover with boiling water and stir with tongs. Let soak for 10 minutes.
- While noodles soak, heat vegetable oil in a pan over medium-high heat. Cook and stir celery, jalapenos, and green onions until tender and fragrant, about 10 minutes.
- Drain noodles and place in the pan; add the sauce and crabmeat. Cook and stir until noodles are coated evenly and everything is heated through, 2 to 3 minutes.

Nutrition Information

- Calories: 669 calories
- Total Fat: 16 g
- Cholesterol: 62 mg
- Sodium: 1982 mg
- Total Carbohydrate: 105.4 g
- Protein: 25.2 g

29. Easy Corn and Crab Chowder

"This is a simple yet flavorful chowder that can be prepared in a jiffy. Chicken curry variation is just as easy, and just as tasty. Leftovers make a great casserole or au gratin the next day."

Serving: 4

Ingredients

- 1 russet potato, peeled and cubed
- 5 slices bacon, diced
- 1/2 onion, chopped
- 1 (6 ounce) can crab meat, drained
- 1/2 teaspoon parsley flakes
- 2 tablespoons butter
- 1/3 cup all-purpose flour
- 1/4 cup dry white wine (optional)
- 1 cube chicken bouillon
- 1 1/2 cups milk
- 1 (15 ounce) can creamed corn
- salt and pepper to taste

Direction

- Wrap potato cubes in plastic wrap, and microwave for 30 seconds. Set aside.
- In a sauté pan, cook bacon over medium heat until heated through, and add chopped onions. Cook and stir until onions are clear. Stir in crab meat and parsley flakes. Set aside.
- Meanwhile, melt butter in a large stock pot over low heat. Whisk in flour until mixture becomes creamy and takes on an

eggshell color. Continue to cook for a few more minutes, stirring occasionally. Stir in wine. Dissolve chicken bouillon in milk; when the flour mixture is crumbly, slowly whisk in the milk. Mix well in order to eliminate all lumps.

- When the mixture is creamy and hot, stir in bacon mixture, cubed potatoes, and creamed corn. Season with salt and pepper to taste, and simmer for 10 minutes.
- For a creamy curry variation add 2 tablespoons curry powder after adding the wine to the flour mixture, and substitute cooked, cubed chicken for the bacon.

Nutrition Information

- Calories: 485 calories
- Total Fat: 24.6 g
- Cholesterol: 84 mg
- Sodium: 1146 mg
- Total Carbohydrate: 45.6 g
- Protein: 20.4 g

30. Easy Tomato Crab Soup

"Quick and easy tomato and seafood cream soup."

Serving: 6 | Prep: 10 m | Cook: 15 m | Ready in: 25 m

Ingredients

- 2 tablespoons olive oil
- 2 cloves garlic, minced
- 1/4 cup chopped onion
- 1 (10.75 ounce) can condensed tomato soup
- 1 (14.5 ounce) can diced tomatoes
- 1 (6 ounce) can crabmeat
- 1 pint half-and-half cream

Direction

- In a large saucepan over medium heat, cook garlic and onion in oil until softened. Stir in tomato soup, tomatoes and crabmeat and heat through. Stir in half-and-half and cook until bubbly.

Nutrition Information

- Calories: 242 calories
- Total Fat: 16.4 g
- Cholesterol: 59 mg
- Sodium: 520 mg
- Total Carbohydrate: 14 g
- Protein: 10.1 g

31. Garlic Oyster Linguini

"This is a popular Cajun appetizer dish."

Serving: 4

Ingredients

- 1/4 cup butter
- 8 ounces fresh mushrooms, quartered
- 1 teaspoon Cajun seasoning
- 1 teaspoon minced garlic
- 24 shucked oysters, quartered
- 1/2 cup whole corn kernels, blanched
- 2/3 cup French-style green beans, chopped
- 2 tablespoons chopped pimento peppers
- 1/2 cup seafood stock
- 10 ounces fresh linguine pasta
- 2 tablespoons butter
- 2 tablespoons all-purpose flour
- 2 tablespoons chopped fresh parsley
- 3 tablespoons thinly sliced green onion
- 4 ounces crabmeat

Direction

- In a small saucepan, melt 2 tablespoons butter or margarine. Stir in flour to make a paste. Set roux aside.
- Sauté mushrooms, Cajun spice, and garlic in 1/4 cup butter or margarine over medium-high heat for 2 minutes. Add oysters, corn, string beans, and pimento. Sauté for 1 1/2 minutes. Add stock and linguine, and bring to a slight simmer.

- Fold in roux until sauce thickens, then reduce heat. Fold in parsley and scallions. Fold in lump crabmeat, and heat through. Serve immediately.

Nutrition Information

- Calories: 497 calories
- Total Fat: 20.7 g
- Cholesterol: 146 mg
- Sodium: 577 mg
- Total Carbohydrate: 51.1 g
- Protein: 27 g

32. Ginas Crab Stuffed Chicken Breast

"Yum!"

Serving: 4 | Prep: 20 m | Cook: 1 h 25 m | Ready in: 1 h 45 m

Ingredients

- 1/4 cup butter
- 1/4 cup all-purpose flour
- 3/4 cup chicken broth
- 3/4 cup milk
- 1/3 cup dry white wine
- 1/4 cup onion, chopped
- 1 cup buttery round crackers, crushed
- 1 (8 ounce) can crabmeat
- 2 tablespoons chopped fresh parsley
- 4 skinless, boneless chicken breast halves
- 1 cup shredded Cheddar cheese

Direction

- To make sauce: melt butter in a saucepan. Stir in flour until smooth, Cook and stir 5 minutes, then gradually stir in broth, milk and white wine. Cook on low until sauce thickens fully, about 20 minutes. Remove from heat and set aside.
- Mix together onion, cracker crumbs, crab meat, parsley, and 1/4 cup of the sauce.
- Pound chicken breasts to 1/4 inch thickness. Spoon 1/4 of the crab mixture on the edge of each chicken breast; roll up. Place

chicken rolls in a lightly greased 9x13 inch baking dish, fold side down, then top with remaining white sauce.
- Cover dish and bake at 350 degrees F (175 degrees C) or until chicken juices run clear, about 1 hour. Sprinkle with cheese and bake, uncovered, until the cheese is lightly browned, about 5 minutes more.

Nutrition Information

- Calories: 797 calories
- Total Fat: 43.4 g
- Cholesterol: 188 mg
- Sodium: 1221 mg
- Total Carbohydrate: 43.4 g
- Protein: 51.6 g

33. Glenns Blowing Rock Salmon

"After eating this at a restaurant in Blowing Rock, North Carolina, I was surprised that the chef was willing to give me the recipe. My favorite way of preparing salmon. A suitable meal for special company. Excellent with Pinot Grigio - our favorite is Ecco Domani®. We usually serve it with baked rice with pine nuts."

Serving: 4 | Prep: 20 m | Cook: 30 m | Ready in: 50 m

Ingredients

- 4 (6 ounce) thick salmon fillets
- 1 (6 ounce) can lump crabmeat, divided
- 4 slices smoked Gouda cheese
- 1/4 cup butter, melted
- 2 lemons, juiced - divided
- 1 (8 ounce) carton sour cream
- 1 tablespoon finely chopped fresh dill
- 1 (2 ounce) jar capers in brine, drained

Direction

- Preheat oven to 350 degrees F (175 degrees C).
- Trim the salmon fillets, if necessary, to remove thin portion; with a very sharp knife, cut the fillets horizontally through the center but leave one end uncut so the fillet opens like a book. Place 1/4 of the lump crabmeat onto each opened fillet, and top crab with a slice of smoked Gouda; close the fillets. Place each fillet into a single-serving baking dish. Mix the melted butter and juice of 1 lemon in a small bowl, and drizzle the lemon butter over all the salmon fillets.

- Bake in the preheated oven until the salmon is opaque and flakes easily, 30 minutes or as needed.
- In a bowl, mix the juice of the 2nd lemon with sour cream and dill; spoon sour cream mixture over each baked fillet, and sprinkle liberally with capers. Serve immediately.

Nutrition Information

- Calories: 607 calories
- Total Fat: 42.5 g
- Cholesterol: 207 mg
- Sodium: 965 mg
- Total Carbohydrate: 5.7 g
- Protein: 49.8 g

34. Hot Crabmeat Dip

"This is a wonderfully creamy and tasty dip, made rich with crabmeat and topped with toasted almonds. Serve it with slices of your favorite bread."

Serving: 16 | Prep: 5 m | Cook: 45 m | Ready in: 50 m

Ingredients

- 1 (8 ounce) package cream cheese, softened
- 1 tablespoon milk
- 2 tablespoons minced onion
- 1 teaspoon prepared horseradish
- 1/4 teaspoon salt
- 1 pinch ground black pepper
- 1 (6 ounce) can crabmeat, drained and flaked
- 1/3 cup sliced almonds

Direction

- Preheat oven to 300 degrees F (150 degrees C).
- In a medium bowl, mix the cream cheese, milk, onion, horseradish, salt, pepper and crabmeat. Spread the mixture into a pie pan or shallow baking dish. Sprinkle almonds over the crabmeat mixture
- Bake in the preheated oven 45 minutes, or until bubbly and lightly browned.

Nutrition Information

- Calories: 78 calories
- Total Fat: 6.6 g

- Cholesterol: 25 mg
- Sodium: 114 mg
- Total Carbohydrate: 1.2 g
- Protein: 3.9 g

35. Janets Appetizer

"Toast topped with a delightful mayonnaise and cheese mixture, with a taste of lemon pepper! It's easy to do ahead, and delectable. The crab is entirely optional but quite delicious!"

Serving: 8 | Prep: 10 m | Cook: 2 m | Ready in: 12 m

Ingredients

- 1 cup mayonnaise
- 1 cup minced red onion
- 1 cup shredded white Cheddar cheese
- 1 cup crabmeat (optional)
- 1 teaspoon Dijon-style prepared mustard
- 1/2 teaspoon garlic powder
- 1/2 (1 pound) loaf sliced pumpernickel party bread
- lemon pepper to taste

Direction

- Preheat your oven's broiler.
- In a medium bowl, stir together mayonnaise, onion, cheddar, crabmeat, mustard, and garlic powder.
- Arrange bread slices on a cookie sheet. Place 1 tablespoon of the mixture on each slice. Sprinkle the bread slice liberally with lemon pepper spice (this is the key ingredient, so don't be shy with the spice!).
- Broil for less than two minutes.

Nutrition Information

- Calories: 357 calories
- Total Fat: 27.6 g
- Cholesterol: 40 mg
- Sodium: 488 mg
- Total Carbohydrate: 17.4 g
- Protein: 10.4 g

36. Joelles Famous Hot Crab and Artichoke Dip

"This hot crab and artichoke dip recipe is the best one around! Very flavorful and a crowd pleaser! Easy to make and mmm good! From a native Marylander who knows her crabs."

Serving: 15 | Prep: 10 m | Cook: 30 m | Ready in: 40 m

Ingredients

- 3 (6 ounce) cans crabmeat
- 1 (8 ounce) package cream cheese, softened
- 1 (8 ounce) container sour cream
- 1 cup mayonnaise
- 1 cup heavy cream
- 1 (10 ounce) can artichoke hearts, drained
- 1 1/2 cups shredded white Cheddar cheese
- 1 tablespoon prepared horseradish
- 2 tablespoons fresh lemon juice
- 2 teaspoons Old Bay Seasoning TM
- 2 tablespoons minced garlic
- ground black pepper to taste
- 2 (1 pound) loaves sourdough bread

Direction

- Preheat oven to 350 degrees F (175 degrees C).
- In a large bowl, combine crabmeat, cream cheese, sour cream, mayonnaise, heavy cream and artichokes. Season with horseradish, lemon juice, garlic, and black pepper. Mix well and

spread mixture into a 9x13 inch baking dish and sprinkle the white Cheddar cheese and Old Bay seasoning on top.
- Bake in a preheated oven for 30 minutes or until warm and melted. Meanwhile, hollow out the loaves of sourdough bread. Reserving the bread removed.
- Spoon the hot crab dip into the hollowed out loaves of sourdough. Use the reserved bread for dipping.

Nutrition Information

- Calories: 520 calories
- Total Fat: 32 g
- Cholesterol: 95 mg
- Sodium: 981 mg
- Total Carbohydrate: 38.7 g
- Protein: 20.2 g

37. Johns Crabby Caps

"Crab stuffed mushrooms with a little extra attitude!"

Serving: 6 | Prep: 20 m | Cook: 15 m | Ready in: 45 m

Ingredients

- 2 cloves garlic, minced
- 1 tablespoon butter
- 1 teaspoon chili powder
- 1 cup grated Parmesan cheese
- 1/3 cup mayonnaise
- 1/4 cup Italian-style seasoned bread crumbs
- salt and pepper to taste
- 2 (6 ounce) cans crabmeat, drained and flaked
- 18 large fresh mushrooms, stems removed
- 1/4 cup cooking sherry

Direction

- Preheat oven to 350 degrees F (175 degrees C).
- In a medium saucepan over medium heat, cook and stir the garlic in the butter until tender.
- In a medium bowl, mix garlic and butter, chili powder, 3/4 cup Parmesan cheese, mayonnaise, Italian-style breadcrumbs, salt and pepper. Increase the amount of mayonnaise, if desired. Fold in the crabmeat.
- Stuff mushroom caps generously with the mixture from the bowl.
- Pour cooking sherry in a large baking dish. Arrange stuffed mushroom caps, stuffing side up, in the baking dish. Top with

remaining Parmesan cheese. Bake 10 minutes in the preheated oven.

- Raise oven temperature to broil. Continue cooking mushrooms 3 to 5 minutes, or until stuffing is bubbly and lightly browned. Allow to cool slightly before serving.

Nutrition Information

- Calories: 277 calories
- Total Fat: 17.5 g
- Cholesterol: 74 mg
- Sodium: 663 mg
- Total Carbohydrate: 8.8 g
- Protein: 20.9 g

38. Key West Crab Salad

"A yummy spinach salad with an orange dressing. Tuna or shrimp can be substituted for the crab meat."

Serving: 4 | Prep: 15 m | Ready in: 15 m

Ingredients

- 3 cups fresh spinach - rinsed, dried and torn into bite-size pieces
- 2 cups leaf lettuce - rinsed, dried and torn into bite-size pieces
- 1 cup finely shredded cabbage
- 2 large oranges, peeled and segmented
- 1 red onion, sliced in rings
- 2 (6 ounce) cans crabmeat
- 1/2 teaspoon orange zest
- 3 tablespoons orange juice
- 2 tablespoons balsamic vinegar
- 2 teaspoons olive oil
- 1 teaspoon fresh chopped tarragon

Direction

- In a large bowl, combine spinach, lettuce, cabbage, oranges, and onions. Add crabmeat, and gently toss until combined. Set aside.
- In a small jar with a tight-fitting lid, combine orange zest, orange juice, vinegar, oil and tarragon. Cover, and shake until well mixed.
- Pour orange dressing over spinach salad, and gently toss until salad is well coated.

Nutrition Information

- Calories: 183 calories
- Total Fat: 3.7 g
- Cholesterol: 75 mg
- Sodium: 312 mg
- Total Carbohydrate: 18.5 g
- Protein: 19.8 g

39. King Crab Appetizers

"These crab tartlets have long since been a family favorite and are requested often at holiday get togethers."

Serving: 12 | Prep: 10 m | Cook: 20 m | Ready in: 30 m

Ingredients

- 2 (12 ounce) packages refrigerated biscuit dough
- 1 (8 ounce) package cream cheese, softened
- 1 (6 ounce) can crab meat, drained
- 2 tablespoons mayonnaise
- 2 tablespoons grated Parmesan cheese
- 1/2 cup shredded Cheddar cheese
- 2 tablespoons thinly sliced green onion
- 1 teaspoon Worcestershire sauce
- 1 pinch paprika

Direction

- Preheat oven to 375 degrees F (190 degrees C). Lightly grease 12 tartlet pans.
- Divide rolls in half and press into the prepared tartlet pans. Set aside.
- In a large bowl, combine cream cheese, crab, mayonnaise, Parmesan cheese, Cheddar cheese, green onions and Worcestershire sauce. Spoon 1 teaspoon of mixture into tarts and garnish with paprika.
- Bake at 375 degrees F (190 degrees C) for 15 to 20 minutes, or until light brown. These freeze wonderfully. Just reheat before serving.

Nutrition Information

- Calories: 299 calories
- Total Fat: 18 g
- Cholesterol: 40 mg
- Sodium: 721 mg
- Total Carbohydrate: 25.1 g
- Protein: 9.6 g

40. Layered Crab Spread

"I'm always requested to bring this quick, easy appetizer to holiday gatherings. It's a little spicier than other crab spreads!"

Serving: 24 | Prep: 10 m | Ready in: 2 h 10 m

Ingredients

- 2 (8 ounce) packages cream cheese, softened
- 2 tablespoons lemon juice
- 1 teaspoon Worcestershire sauce
- 1/4 teaspoon garlic powder
- 2 tablespoons finely chopped onion
- 1 tablespoon dried parsley
- 1 (12 ounce) bottle chili sauce
- 1 (6 ounce) can crabmeat, drained and flaked

Direction

- In a large bowl, beat together cream cheese, lemon juice, Worcestershire sauce, garlic powder and onion. Stir in the parsley. Spread the mixture evenly on a large serving platter. Layer with desired amount of chili sauce. Top with crabmeat. Cover and chill in the refrigerator at least two hours before serving.

Nutrition Information

- Calories: 75 calories
- Total Fat: 6.6 g
- Cholesterol: 27 mg

- Sodium: 99 mg
- Total Carbohydrate: 1.1 g
- Protein: 2.9 g

41. Loris Famous Crab Cakes

"These crab cakes are just the best. I make these often at home, and I make a smaller appetizer size for parties. They are always a hit. They are easy and delicious. I won't eat crab cakes out anymore! Serve with fresh squeezed lemon and tartar sauce!"

Serving: 6 | Prep: 25 m | Cook: 20 m | Ready in: 45 m

Ingredients

- 1/3 cup dry bread crumbs
- 1/4 green bell pepper, seeded and diced
- 1/4 red bell pepper, seeded and diced
- 2 green onions, thinly sliced
- 4 sprigs fresh parsley, chopped
- 1/2 teaspoon hot pepper sauce
- 1 egg white
- 2 tablespoons mayonnaise
- 1 tablespoon fresh lemon juice
- 1/2 teaspoon Worcestershire sauce
- 2 teaspoons Dijon mustard
- 1/4 teaspoon Old Bay TM seasoning
- 1/4 teaspoon dry mustard
- 1/4 teaspoon onion powder
- 3 (6 ounce) cans crabmeat, drained and flaked
- 1/2 cup dry bread crumbs
- 1 cup canola oil for frying

Direction

- In a bowl, toss together the 1/3 cup bread crumbs, green bell pepper, red bell pepper, green onions, and parsley. Mix in the egg white, mayonnaise, lemon juice, Worcestershire sauce, and Dijon mustard. Season with Old Bay seasoning, dry mustard, and onion powder. Fold crabmeat into the mixture. Form into 6 large cakes. Coat in the remaining 1/2 cup bread crumbs.
- Heat the oil in a large, heavy skillet. Fry the cakes 5 minutes on each side, or until evenly brown. Drain on paper towels.

Nutrition Information

- Calories: 225 calories
- Total Fat: 9.4 g
- Cholesterol: 77 mg
- Sodium: 508 mg
- Total Carbohydrate: 13.8 g
- Protein: 20.7 g

42. Maryland Crab Cakes I

"Growing up near the Chesapeake Bay you learn that crabs are as valuable as gold. My mom made crab cakes every Friday in the summer months, but I like my recipe just a tad better. Don't tell mom."

Serving: 6 | Prep: 12 m | Cook: 8 m | Ready in: 20 m

Ingredients

- 1 pound crabmeat
- 2 slices white bread, crusts trimmed
- 1 egg, beaten
- 1 tablespoon mayonnaise
- 1 teaspoon Dijon-style prepared mustard
- 1 teaspoon Worcestershire sauce
- 1 tablespoon Old Bay Seasoning TM
- 2 tablespoons butter

Direction

- Pick the crab meat to remove any remaining pieces of shell.
- Pick bread into small pieces and place in medium-size bowl with crabmeat. Add egg, mayonnaise, mustard, Worcestershire sauce, and Old Bay seasoning (tm). Mix ingredients by hand to avoid overworking the crabmeat, you want to keep the lumps of meat as much as possible. Form into patties; this should make 6 good-size cakes.
- Heat 2 tablespoons of butter in a skillet, then fry cakes for about 4 minutes each side or until brown crust forms on both sides of the crab cake.

Nutrition Information

- Calories: 166 calories
- Total Fat: 7.9 g
- Cholesterol: 114 mg
- Sodium: 896 mg
- Total Carbohydrate: 5.3 g
- Protein: 17.4 g

43. Maryland Crab Cakes II

"Maryland is famous for its crab cakes! After you've tried this recipe, you'll know why."

Serving: 4 | Prep: 15 m | Cook: 20 m | Ready in: 35 m

Ingredients

- 1 pound crabmeat, shredded
- 1 1/2 tablespoons dry bread crumbs
- 2 teaspoons chopped fresh parsley
- salt and pepper to taste
- 1 egg
- 1 1/2 tablespoons mayonnaise
- 1/2 teaspoon ground dry mustard
- 1 dash hot pepper sauce

Direction

- Preheat oven broiler.
- Mix together crabmeat, bread crumbs, parsley, salt and pepper.
- Beat together egg, mayonnaise, hot sauce and mustard. Combine with other ingredients and mix well. Form into patties and place on a lightly greased broiler pan or baking sheet.
- Broil for 10 to 15 minutes, until lightly brown.

Nutrition Information

- Calories: 211 calories
- Total Fat: 13 g
- Cholesterol: 185 mg

- Sodium: 373 mg
- Total Carbohydrate: 2.6 g
- Protein: 20.1 g

44. Micheles Crab and Shrimp Imperial

"This is crab imperial with a shrimp paste added. It makes the texture of the dish, more like a spongy crabcake. Every time I make it, people just love it. "

Serving: 8 | Prep: 20 m | Cook: 30 m | Ready in: 50 m

Ingredients

- 1 serving cooking spray (optional)
- 2 pounds peeled and deveined extra-large shrimp
- 2 extra-large eggs
- 3/4 cup mayonnaise
- 1 tablespoon prepared yellow mustard
- 3 dashes hot pepper sauce
- 2 teaspoons seafood seasoning (such as Old Bay®)
- 1 tablespoon dried tarragon
- salt and pepper to taste
- 2 (6 ounce) cans crabmeat, drained

Direction

- Preheat oven to 350 degrees F (175 degrees C). Coat an 8x8 inch baking dish with nonstick cooking spray.
- Place shrimp in the work bowl of a food processor; pulse until shrimp forms a thick paste. Mix eggs, mayonnaise, mustard, hot pepper sauce, seafood seasoning, dried tarragon, and salt and pepper in a large bowl. Stir in shrimp; carefully fold in crab. Spoon into prepared baking dish.

- Bake in preheated oven until lightly browned and heated through, about 30 minutes.

Nutrition Information

- Calories: 303 calories
- Total Fat: 19.4 g
- Cholesterol: 272 mg
- Sodium: 645 mg
- Total Carbohydrate: 1.3 g
- Protein: 29.4 g

45. Moqueca Baiana Brazilian Seafood Stew

"Moqueca baiana is a rich seafood stew from Brazil, reminiscent of a mild curry but not made from a spice paste base. This recipe is for the Afro-Brazilian version of moqueca from the state of Bahia. There's also moqueca capixaba from Espirito Santo which uses tomato puree and annatto, lacking the African influence by omitting the coconut milk and dende oil (palm oil). Dende oil is the key ingredient in this recipe."

Serving: 8 | Prep: 40 m | Cook: 48 m | Ready in: 1 h 28 m

Ingredients

- 1 (16 ounce) can crabmeat
- 1/2 pound cooked shrimp, peeled and deveined without tail
- 3 tablespoons lemon juice
- 1 tablespoon lime juice
- 3 cloves garlic, minced
- 1 teaspoon salt, divided
- 1 teaspoon freshly ground black pepper, divided
- 2 1/2 cups uncooked long-grain white rice
- 3 cups water
- 2 tablespoons water
- 1 (14 ounce) can coconut milk
- 1 yellow onion, coarsely chopped
- 2 1/2 tablespoons butter
- 2 teaspoons salt
- 1 clove garlic
- 2 tablespoons dende oil (palm oil)
- 1 yellow onion, sliced
- 1 small yellow bell pepper, seeded and sliced
- 1 small orange bell pepper, seeded and sliced

- 1 teaspoon crushed red pepper
- 3 Roma tomatoes, sliced
- 1 Roma tomato, chopped
- 1/2 cup chopped green onions
- 1/2 cup chopped fresh cilantro

Direction

- Place crabmeat and shrimp in a dish; coat with lemon juice, lime juice, 3 cloves garlic, 1/2 teaspoon salt, and 1/2 teaspoon black pepper. Mix well. Cover with plastic wrap; chill until ready to use.
- Combine rice, 3 cups plus 2 tablespoons water, coconut milk, chopped onion, butter, 2 teaspoons salt, and 1 clove garlic in a large saucepan or rice cooker. Simmer, covered, until water is absorbed, about 15 minutes.
- Heat dende oil in a large skillet over medium heat. Cook and stir sliced onion until beginning to soften, about 5 minutes. Add yellow bell pepper, orange bell pepper, and crushed pepper. Cook and stir until heated through, 3 to 5 minutes. Add sliced tomatoes, chopped tomato, and green onions. Reduce heat to low; let vegetable mixture simmer for 5 minutes. Add the remaining 1/2 teaspoon salt, 1/2 teaspoon black pepper, and cilantro.
- Transfer 1/2 the vegetable mixture to a plate. Spread the remaining mixture to evenly cover the bottom of the skillet. Spread crab-shrimp mixture on top. Top with the remaining vegetable mixture and pour on coconut milk. Bring to a simmer over medium heat. Reduce heat to low. Cook without stirring until flavors blend, about 15 minutes. Serve over the rice.

Nutrition Information

- Calories: 480 calories
- Total Fat: 18.9 g
- Cholesterol: 96 mg
- Sodium: 1139 mg
- Total Carbohydrate: 57.3 g
- Protein: 21.8 g

46. **Mushrooms Mornay**

"A deliciously rich casserole chock full of crab, mushrooms and sharp Cheddar cheese. Delicious over puff pastry shells or simple toast points. Imitation crabmeat can be substituted, but there is nothing like the real thing!"

Serving: 12 | Prep: 10 m | Cook: 30 m | Ready in: 40 m

Ingredients

- 12 ounces fresh mushrooms, stems removed
- 1 tablespoon vegetable oil
- 1 (6 ounce) can crabmeat
- 2 teaspoons fresh lemon juice
- 3 tablespoons butter
- 3 tablespoons all-purpose flour
- 1 1/4 cups milk
- 2 egg yolks
- 6 ounces sharp Cheddar cheese, shredded
- 2 tablespoons cooking sherry

Direction

- Preheat oven to broil. Place mushroom caps on a baking sheet, and brush with oil. Broil until soft and slightly browned.
- Meanwhile, melt butter in a saucepan over medium heat. Stir in flour to make a paste. Whisk in milk; cook, stirring frequently, until hot. In a small bowl, beat egg yolks together, then pour a small amount of the hot milk mixture into the yolks. Whisk this yolk mixture into milk in saucepan. Remove from heat, and stir in 1 1/4 cups cheese.
- Preheat oven to 350 degrees F (175 degrees C).

- Place mushroom caps, hollow side up, in an 8 inch, round baking dish. Cover with crab, and sprinkle with lemon juice. Pour cheese sauce over mushrooms and crab, and top with remaining 1/4 cup cheese.
- Bake in preheated oven for 20 minutes, or until hot and bubbly.

Nutrition Information

- Calories: 144 calories
- Total Fat: 10.3 g
- Cholesterol: 71 mg
- Sodium: 183 mg
- Total Carbohydrate: 4.3 g
- Protein: 8.8 g

47. My Crab Cakes

"Great crab cakes with lots of flavor and spice. Serve with homemade aioli and a crisp white wine!"

Serving: 10 | Prep: 20 m | Cook: 10 m | Ready in: 30 m

Ingredients

- 2 tablespoons olive oil
- 6 green onions, chopped
- 3/8 cup olive oil
- 1 (16 ounce) can canned crabmeat, drained
- 1 egg
- 1 tablespoon mayonnaise
- 1 teaspoon dry mustard
- 8 ounces buttery round crackers, crushed
- 1/2 teaspoon ground cayenne pepper
- 1 teaspoon garlic powder
- 1/4 teaspoon Old Bay Seasoning TM
- salt to taste
- ground black pepper to taste
- 1 cup panko (Japanese bread crumbs) or regular dry bread crumbs

Direction

- Heat 2 tablespoons oil in a skillet over high heat. Sauté green onions briefly until tender; cool slightly.
- Combine crabmeat, sautéed green onions, egg, mayonnaise, dry mustard, crushed crackers, cayenne pepper, garlic powder,

Old Bay seasoning, salt and pepper. Form into 1/2 inch thick patties. Coat the patties with bread crumbs.

- Heat 1/2 cup oil in a skillet over medium high heat. Cook cakes until golden brown on each side. Drain briefly on paper towels and serve hot.

Nutrition Information

- Calories: 318 calories
- Total Fat: 22.1 g
- Cholesterol: 73 mg
- Sodium: 407 mg
- Total Carbohydrate: 22 g
- Protein: 10.5 g

48. New England Crab Cakes

"This recipe comes from Maine and is EXCELLENT! These cakes are so yummy they almost melt in your mouth! They're great served with a seafood pasta salad, boiled potatoes, or fresh steamed veggies. "

Serving: 4 | Prep: 10 m | Cook: 10 m | Ready in: 20 m

Ingredients

- 1 pound crabmeat
- 1/2 cup dry bread crumbs
- 1 egg, beaten
- 1 tablespoon mayonnaise
- 1 teaspoon prepared Dijon-style mustard
- 1 teaspoon Worcestershire sauce
- 1 tablespoon Old Bay Seasoning TM
- 2 tablespoons butter

Direction

- In a medium size bowl, combine the bread crumbs and the crab meat. Stir the beaten egg, mayonnaise, mustard, Worcestershire and Old Bay Seasoning. Lightly mix these ingredients being careful not to overwork the crab meat. Form into 8 round, flat crab cakes.
- Heat butter in a skillet over medium heat. Fry the cakes on each side until crusty and golden brown. Serve warm.

Nutrition Information

- Calories: 452 calories

- Total Fat: 28.4 g
- Cholesterol: 172 mg
- Sodium: 1277 mg
- Total Carbohydrate: 26.6 g
- Protein: 21.8 g

49. OldSchool Baltimore Crab Soup

"This crab soup recipe mirrors the traditional crab soups made by Baltimore women over the last 50 years. It is a milder-flavored, lighter-colored soup than the ones typically served in modern seafood restaurants. Homemade crab soup is a staple at most Maryland cookouts and family gatherings. Serve with crackers."

Serving: 12 | Prep: 25 m | Cook: 4 h | Ready in: 4 h 25 m

Ingredients

- 3 carrots, sliced
- 1 ham bone
- 2/3 cup barley
- 2 tablespoons salt, or more to taste
- 2 tablespoons ground black pepper, or more to taste
- 4 cups water
- 1 small head cabbage, shredded
- 2 (14.5 ounce) cans diced tomatoes
- 3 potatoes, peeled and cubed
- 1 cup water
- 3 (15 ounce) cans white corn, drained
- 1 pound green beans, cut into 1 inch pieces
- 1 (10 ounce) package frozen lima beans
- 1 (6 ounce) package frozen peas
- 2 tablespoons seafood seasoning (such as Old Bay®), or more to taste
- 4 female blue crabs
- 4 slices bacon
- 1 cup water
- 2 (6 ounce) cans lump crabmeat, drained

Direction

- Bring a large pot of lightly salted water to a boil. Add the carrots, and cook uncovered until tender, about 5 minutes. Drain well, and set aside.
- Place the ham bone, barley, salt, and pepper in large stock pot with 4 cups of water. Simmer over medium heat for 30 to 45 minutes. Add cabbage and tomatoes; continue simmering for 15 more minutes. Stir in the potatoes and carrots. Simmer until the potatoes are tender and easily pierced with a fork, 20 to 30 minutes. Stir in 1 cup of water, corn, green beans, lima beans, and peas. Simmer for 20 minutes.
- While the soup is simmering, clean the crabs by opening it and discarding the lungs and mouth. Remove the yellowish-brown tomalley and set aside. Break the crabs in half and add to the soup along with the seafood seasoning. Simmer for 20 minutes, stirring occasionally.
- Meanwhile, place the bacon in a large, deep skillet, and cook over medium-high heat, turning occasionally, until evenly browned, about 10 minutes. Drain the bacon slices on a paper towel-lined plate. Cook and stir the reserved tomalley in the remaining bacon grease over low heat until the mixture becomes gravy-like. Stir the cooked tomalley into the soup with 1 more cup of water. Continue simmering for 45 minutes, then add the lump crabmeat. Season with additional salt, pepper, and seafood seasoning, if necessary. Simmer for 1 hour and 15 minutes, stirring occasionally. Reduce heat to low, until ready to serve.

Nutrition Information

- Calories: 350 calories

- Total Fat: 3.5 g
- Cholesterol: 34 mg
- Sodium: 2079 mg
- Total Carbohydrate: 64.3 g
- Protein: 21.1 g

50. **Portabella Nirvana**

"Roasted portobello mushrooms are stuffed with a savory crab stuffing like a gigantic appetizer. If this isn't Heaven, your taste buds will be there anyway!"

Serving: 4 | Prep: 20 m | Cook: 30 m | Ready in: 50 m

Ingredients

- 2 large portobello mushrooms
- 1 (8 ounce) bottle Italian-style salad dressing
- 1 tablespoon minced onion
- 1 1/2 teaspoons minced garlic
- 1/4 cup butter
- 1 stalk celery, diced
- 1/2 cup crab meat, fresh or canned
- 20 buttery round crackers, crushed
- 2/3 cup Italian blend shredded cheese, divided

Direction

- Preheat your oven's broiler. Clean mushrooms, and remove stems, reserving them for later. Marinate the mushroom caps in Italian dressing for 15 minutes. Remove from marinade, and place into a baking dish.
- Broil at least 6 inches from heat for about 10 minutes. Check occasionally to make sure they do not burn. Turn off the broiler, and preheat the oven to 400 degrees F (200 degrees C).
- Melt butter in a skillet over medium-high heat. Chop reserved mushroom stems. Sautee onion, garlic, mushroom stems and celery until tender. Add the crabmeat, and heat until cooked through, about 5 minutes. Transfer the skillet mixture to a

medium bowl, and mix in crackers, 1/3 cup of the cheese blend, and mix until well blended. Use some of the Italian dressing marinade to hold the mixture together if necessary. Pack the crab mixture into the cavities of the mushrooms. Season with salt and pepper to taste.

- Bake for 10 minutes in the preheated oven. Remove from the oven, and sprinkle remaining cheese over the tops, then return to the oven for 3 minutes, or until cheese has melted.

Nutrition Information

- Calories: 455 calories
- Total Fat: 37.6 g
- Cholesterol: 60 mg
- Sodium: 1387 mg
- Total Carbohydrate: 20.6 g
- Protein: 10.9 g

51. Savannah Seafood Stuffing

"This is a seafood stuffing that has been in my family for a while. We have never actually stuffed the bird with this to avoid the turkey having a 'fishy' taste. We tend to like our dressing very moist, but if you prefer a drier stuffing, only use half of the broth."

Serving: 8 | Prep: 20 m | Cook: 30 m | Ready in: 50 m

Ingredients

- 1/2 cup margarine
- 1/2 cup chopped green bell pepper
- 1/2 cup chopped onion
- 1/2 cup chopped celery
- 1 pound crabmeat, drained and flaked
- 1/2 pound medium shrimp - peeled and deveined
- 1/2 cup seasoned dry bread crumbs
- 1 (6 ounce) package corn bread stuffing mix
- 2 tablespoons white sugar, divided
- 1 (10.75 ounce) can condensed cream of mushroom soup
- 1 (14.5 ounce) can chicken broth

Direction

- Melt the margarine in a large skillet over medium heat. Add the bell pepper, onion, celery crabmeat and shrimp; cook and stir for about 5 minutes. Set aside. In a large bowl, stir together the stuffing, bread crumbs and 1 tablespoon of sugar. Mix in the vegetables and seafood from the skillet. Stir in the cream of mushroom soup and as much of the chicken broth as you like. Spoon into a 9x13 inch baking dish.

- Bake for 30 minutes in the preheated oven, or until lightly toasted on top.

Nutrition Information

- Calories: 344 calories
- Total Fat: 15.7 g
- Cholesterol: 94 mg
- Sodium: 1141 mg
- Total Carbohydrate: 28.4 g
- Protein: 22 g

52. Seafood Alfredo Dip

"This easy recipe makes an impressive dip for any party, as well as a great topping for flat iron steak or almost any type of baked fish."

Serving: 12 | Prep: 5 m | Cook: 10 m | Ready in: 15 m

Ingredients

- 3 tablespoons butter
- 2 tablespoons all-purpose flour
- 1 cup heavy cream
- 2 (4 ounce) cans shrimp, drained
- 1 (6 ounce) can crabmeat, drained
- 1/4 cup shredded Parmesan cheese
- 1/2 teaspoon salt
- 1/8 teaspoon white pepper

Direction

- Melt the butter in a pan over medium heat. Whisk in the flour, and cook to make a smooth paste, about 5 minutes. Gradually stir in the heavy cream. Continue to whisk the mixture until thick and smooth, about 5 minutes. Stir in the shrimp and crabmeat. Add the Parmesan cheese, and stir until melted. Season to taste with salt and white pepper. Serve warm as a dip.

Nutrition Information

- Calories: 144 calories
- Total Fat: 11.4 g

- Cholesterol: 81 mg
- Sodium: 235 mg
- Total Carbohydrate: 1.8 g
- Protein: 8.6 g

53. Seafood File Gumbo

"This is a big recipe and a big time-consumer, but delicious! Serve gumbo over 1/3 cup cooked rice per serving in bowls."

Serving: 8 | Prep: 25 m | Cook: 8 h 50 m | Ready in: 9 h 25 m

Ingredients

- 1 pound shrimp, peeled and deveined
- 5 quarts water
- 4 carrots, sliced
- 4 onions, quartered
- 1/2 bunch celery, sliced
- 2 bay leaves
- 3 cloves garlic, sliced
- 2 sprigs fresh parsley
- 5 whole cloves
- 1 teaspoon ground black pepper
- 1 tablespoon dried basil
- 2 teaspoons dried thyme
- 1/2 teaspoon ground cayenne pepper
- 1/2 tablespoon ground white pepper
- 1/2 teaspoon ground black pepper
- 1 1/2 teaspoons paprika
- 1/2 teaspoon dried thyme
- 1/2 teaspoon dried oregano
- 16 ounces crabmeat
- 1 bay leaf, crushed
- 1 teaspoon salt
- 3/4 cup corn oil
- 2 cups diced onion
- 2 cups diced celery

- 2 cups chopped green bell pepper
- 1 teaspoon minced garlic
- 3 tablespoons file powder
- 2 teaspoons hot pepper sauce
- 1 1/2 cups tomato sauce
- 1 pint shucked oysters

Direction

- Preheat oven to 375 degrees F (190 degrees C).
- Shell and devein the shrimp, reserve the shells. Place the shrimp in a covered bowl and refrigerate. Place the shells on a cookie sheet, and bake until the shells are dried and starting to brown on the edges. Turn off the oven.
- Make the stock: In a 8 quart pot, put 5 quarts of water, 4 carrots, 4 onions, and celery. Add 2 bay leaves, sliced garlic, parsley, cloves, 1 teaspoons black pepper, 1 tablespoon dried basil and 2 teaspoons dried thyme. Add the shrimp shells. Bring the stock slowly to boil. Reduce heat to a gentle simmer and cook 5 to 7 hours, replacing water as needed, 2 or 3 times, by pouring more water down side of pot.
- Remove stock from heat and strain. Press all liquid from the shells and vegetables, then discard them. Return liquid to heat and reduce stock to 2 to 3 quarts, or to your desired quantity (you will need 7 cups of this stock for this recipe). If clarity is desired, strain the stock through a cloth.
- In a small bowl, combine the ground red, white, and black peppers, paprika, thyme, oregano, bay leaf and salt and set aside.
- In a heavy pot, 5-quart or larger, heat oil over medium heat, warming the pot first. Add onions, celery and green pepper. Turn heat to high. Stirring frequently, add garlic, file, hot pepper sauce, and the pepper-herb mixture. Cook for 5 minutes,

stirring constantly. Add tomato sauce and stir as it reduces over high heat. Add 7 cups of the stock and bring to a boil. Reduce heat and simmer for 1 hour, stirring occasionally.

- When ready to serve, add shrimp, oysters, and crabmeat. Cover and wait 5 minutes. Turn off heat and let stand for 10 minutes.

Nutrition Information

- Calories: 418 calories
- Total Fat: 23.6 g
- Cholesterol: 142 mg
- Sodium: 951 mg
- Total Carbohydrate: 24 g
- Protein: 28.8 g

54. Seafood Lasagna II

"I improved on a friends recipe...now it is the best I ever cooked or tasted!"

Serving: 8 | Prep: 30 m | Cook: 1 h | Ready in: 1 h 30 m

Ingredients

- 9 lasagna noodles
- 1 tablespoon butter
- 1 cup minced onion
- 1 (8 ounce) package cream cheese, softened
- 1 1/2 cups cottage cheese
- 1 egg, beaten
- 2 teaspoons dried basil leaves
- 1/2 teaspoon salt
- 1/8 teaspoon freshly ground black pepper
- 2 (10.75 ounce) cans condensed cream of mushroom soup
- 1/3 cup milk
- 1/3 cup dry white wine
- 1 (6 ounce) can crabmeat, drained and flaked
- 1 pound cooked small shrimp
- 1/4 cup grated Parmesan cheese
- 1/2 cup shredded sharp Cheddar cheese

Direction

- Bring a pot of lightly salted water to a boil. Cook pasta for 8 to 10 minutes, or until al dente; drain, and rinse in cold water. Preheat oven to 350 degrees F (175 degrees C).
- In a skillet, cook onion in butter over medium heat until tender. Remove from heat, and stir in cream cheese, cottage cheese,

egg, basil, and salt and pepper.

- In a medium bowl, mix together the soup, milk, wine, crabmeat, and shrimp.
- Lay 3 cooked lasagna noodles on the bottom of a 9x13 inch baking dish. Spread 1/3 of the onion mixture over the noodles. Then spread 1/3 of the soup mixture over the onion layer. Repeat the noodle, onion, soup layers twice more. Top with Cheddar cheese and Parmesan cheese.
- Bake in preheated oven for 45 minutes, or until heated through and bubbly.

Nutrition Information

- Calories: 471 calories
- Total Fat: 23.5 g
- Cholesterol: 206 mg
- Sodium: 1205 mg
- Total Carbohydrate: 29.9 g
- Protein: 33 g

55. Seafood Melange

"Even when prepared for two, this erotic combination of four seafoods encourages a lusty appetite! Light some candles and decant some wine!"

Serving: 2 | Prep: 10 m | Cook: 10 m | Ready in: 30 m

Ingredients

- 4 sole, patted dry
- 10 bay scallops, raw
- 3/4 cup crabmeat
- 3/4 cup cooked shrimp
- 1/2 cup shredded Monterey Jack cheese
- 1/2 cup butter
- 2 egg yolks
- 1 tablespoon lemon juice
- 1/2 teaspoon mustard powder
- 1/8 teaspoon salt
- 2 tablespoons chopped fresh parsley
- 1/4 teaspoon paprika

Direction

- Butter two 2-cup au gratin dishes. Place 1 fillet on bottom of each, then layer with scallops, crabmeat, shrimp, cheese and a second fillet; set aside.
- Preheat oven to 450 degrees F (230 degrees C).
- Melt butter. In a medium mixing bowl, combine yolks, lemon juice, mustard and salt; mix on high and slowly add butter in a steady stream until sauce is thick and creamy. Pour sauce over fillets.

- Bake in preheated oven for 10 to 15 minutes; sprinkle with parsley and paprika. Serve.

Nutrition Information

- Calories: 1202 calories
- Total Fat: 87.9 g
- Cholesterol: 549 mg
- Sodium: 1945 mg
- Total Carbohydrate: 47 g
- Protein: 62.1 g

56. Seafood PeaAsta Salad

"This is a quick and easy recipe and oh-so-tasty!"

Serving: 6

Ingredients

- 1/2 cup mayonnaise
- 1/4 cup Italian-style salad dressing
- 2 tablespoons grated Parmesan cheese
- 2 cups black-eyed peas, rinsed and drained
- 8 ounces fusilli pasta
- 1 cup crabmeat
- 1 cup broccoli florets, parboiled
- 1/2 cup chopped green bell pepper
- 1/2 cup chopped tomatoes
- 1/4 cup chopped green onions

Direction

- Bring a large pot of salted water to a boil. Add pasta and cook for time indicated on package. Drain, rinse and set aside.
- In a large bowl, combine mayonnaise, Italian dressing and cheese and blend well.
- Add peas, pasta, crabmeat, broccoli, pepper, tomato and onions. Toss gently to mix. Cover and refrigerate for at least 2 hours.

Nutrition Information

- Calories: 397 calories
- Total Fat: 19.5 g
- Cholesterol: 28 mg
- Sodium: 614 mg
- Total Carbohydrate: 42.2 g
- Protein: 15 g

57. Seafood Salad

"I have made this for over 20 years--people still always ask me to make it! I vary it a little and it still tastes new."

Serving: 6 | Prep: 30 m | Cook: 10 m | Ready in: 4 h

Ingredients

- 1 (16 ounce) package seashell pasta
- 1 (6 ounce) can crabmeat
- 1 (5 ounce) can tuna
- 1 (4 ounce) can shrimp
- 3 carrots, grated
- 1 onion, grated
- 1 cup creamy salad dressing (e.g. Miracle Whip)
- 1/2 cup French dressing
- 1/2 cup milk
- 4 tablespoons white sugar

Direction

- Bring a large pot of lightly salted water to a boil. Add pasta and cook for 8 to 10 minutes or until al dente; drain.
- In a large mixing bowl, combine cooked pasta, crabmeat, tuna, shrimp, carrots, and onion.
- In a separate small mixing bowl, combine creamy salad dressing, French dressing, milk, and sugar. Pour dressing mixture over pasta mixture and toss well. Refrigerate until well chilled, or overnight.

Nutrition Information

- Calories: 634 calories
- Total Fat: 24.1 g
- Cholesterol: 78 mg
- Sodium: 688 mg
- Total Carbohydrate: 77.2 g
- Protein: 26.5 g

58. Shrimp and Crabmeat Loaf

"This is the best seafood salad spread I've had in ages! It's great for summer or in the winter, you can heat it like a 'melt' sandwich."

Serving: 8 | Prep: 10 m | Cook: 20 m | Ready in: 30 m

Ingredients

- 1 (6 ounce) can small shrimp, drained
- 1 (6 ounce) can crabmeat, drained and flaked
- 1/2 cup mayonnaise
- 1/4 cup thinly sliced green onions
- 1/4 cup diced celery
- 1 (8 ounce) package shredded mozzarella cheese
- 1/8 teaspoon salt
- 1/8 teaspoon ground black pepper
- 1 (1 pound) loaf French bread, halved horizontally

Direction

- In a bowl, combine well the shrimp, crab, mayonnaise, green onions, celery, cheese, salt, and pepper.
- Spread the shrimp mixture on the bottom half of bread and replace the top half. Cut into 8 pieces and serve immediately or refrigerate whole and cut into 8 pieces when ready to serve.
- Heating instructions: Preheat oven to 400 degrees F (200 degrees C). Wrap the loaf in a large piece of aluminum foil. Bake for 20 minutes or until heated through. Cut into 8 pieces.

Nutrition Information

- Calories: 379 calories
- Total Fat: 17.1 g
- Cholesterol: 78 mg
- Sodium: 760 mg
- Total Carbohydrate: 33.4 g
- Protein: 22.7 g

59. Shrimp Wellington

"Shrimp stuffed with crabmeat and spinach, wrapped in puff pastry and baked in the oven. A wonderful appetizer or great served with a well-cut steak."

Serving: 4 | Prep: 15 m | Cook: 20 m | Ready in: 35 m

Ingredients

- 2 tablespoons olive oil
- 4 cups fresh spinach leaves
- salt and pepper to taste
- 1 sheet frozen puff pastry, thawed
- 4 jumbo shrimp, peeled and deveined
- 4 ounces crabmeat, drained and flaked
- 1/4 cup bechamel sauce
- 1 tablespoon chopped shallots
- 1 tablespoon chopped fresh tarragon
- 1 egg, beaten

Direction

- Preheat oven to 400 degrees F (200 degrees C). Grease a baking sheet
- Heat oil in a large skillet over medium heat. Add spinach; cook and stir until wilted, about 3 minutes. Season with salt and pepper. Drain off any excess liquid; set aside.
- Lay the sheet of puff pastry out on a clean surface, and cut into 4 squares. Prick lightly with fork.
- In a medium bowl; mix crabmeat, bechamel sauce, shallots, and tarragon until well blended.

- Cut prawns lengthwise and open them up to form a butterfly shape. Lay one shrimp in the middle of each pastry square with open side facing up. Stuff each shrimp with an equal amount of spinach and top with a heaping tablespoon of the crab mixture. Fold over pastry to make a triangle, and press the edges to seal. Place on the baking sheet, and brush with beaten egg.
- Bake in preheated oven until golden brown, 15 to 20 minutes. Serve warm.

Nutrition Information

- Calories: 502 calories
- Total Fat: 33.5 g
- Cholesterol: 129 mg
- Sodium: 482 mg
- Total Carbohydrate: 30 g
- Protein: 20.1 g

60. Soundview Crab Salad

"Crab salad perfect for spreading on crackers."

Serving: 8 | Prep: 12 m | Ready in: 1 h 12 m

Ingredients

- 2 tablespoons sour cream
- 2 tablespoons mayonnaise
- 2 tablespoons sweet pickle relish
- 1 large shallot, minced
- 1 1/2 teaspoons Worcestershire sauce
- 3/4 teaspoon dried dill weed
- 1/2 teaspoon chopped fresh parsley
- 1/4 teaspoon cayenne pepper
- 1/4 teaspoon paprika
- 1/4 teaspoon fresh lemon juice
- 1/4 teaspoon grated lemon zest
- freshly ground black pepper to taste
- 1 pound crabmeat - drained, flaked and cartilage removed

Direction

- In a large bowl, stir together the sour cream, mayonnaise, relish, shallot, and Worcestershire sauce. Season with dill, parsley, cayenne, paprika, lemon juice, lemon zest, and black pepper; mix until well blended. Stir in crabmeat until evenly coated. Cover and refrigerate for at least an hour before serving to blend flavors.

Nutrition Information

- Calories: 100 calories
- Total Fat: 4.2 g
- Cholesterol: 53 mg
- Sodium: 252 mg
- Total Carbohydrate: 3.1 g
- Protein: 12 g

61. Southwestern Crabcakes

"There is a wonderful hint of the Southwest in these crab-meat filled cakes. Fabulous, healthy dinner that is great served with sour cream, salsa and a side salad."

Serving: 10 | Prep: 15 m | Cook: 15 m | Ready in: 30 m

Ingredients

- 1/2 cup reduced-fat sour cream
- 1 egg white, beaten
- 1/2 cup canned yellow corn
- 1/2 cup minced poblano pepper
- 1 teaspoon chili powder
- 1 teaspoon ground cumin
- 1/4 teaspoon cayenne pepper
- 3/4 cup soft bread crumbs
- 1 (16 ounce) can lump crabmeat, drained
- 1/4 cup olive oil, or as needed

Direction

- In a large bowl, stir together the sour cream and egg white. Stir in the corn and poblano pepper, and season with chili powder, cumin, and cayenne pepper. Mix in the bread crumbs and crabmeat until well blended. Shape into 10 patties about 1/2 inch thick.
- Heat the oil in a large skillet over medium-high heat. Cook the crab cakes 4 or 5 at a time until browned on both sides, about 10 minutes. Cover the pan with a lid while frying so the patties

get heated through. Drain on paper towels, and serve immediately.

Nutrition Information

- Calories: 129 calories
- Total Fat: 7.7 g
- Cholesterol: 45 mg
- Sodium: 211 mg
- Total Carbohydrate: 4.4 g
- Protein: 10.6 g

62. Special Day Crab Mold

"I bring this crab mold every Christmas and it doesn't last long. I have served it with saltine crackers and cocktail rye bread, but you can use whatever you'd like."

Serving: 16 | Prep: 15 m | Cook: 5 m | Ready in: 4 h 20 m

Ingredients

- 1 cup chopped celery
- 4 green onions, chopped
- 2 (6 ounce) cans crabmeat, drained and flaked
- 1 (.25 ounce) envelope unflavored gelatin
- 3 tablespoons cold water
- 1 (10.75 ounce) can cream of chicken soup
- 1 (8 ounce) package cream cheese, softened
- 1 cup mayonnaise
- 1 teaspoon Worcestershire sauce, or to taste
- 1 dash hot pepper sauce (such as Tabasco®), or to taste

Direction

- Process celery, green onions, and crab in a food processor until finely chopped, about 30 seconds. Sprinkle gelatin over cold water in a small bowl; let stand until softened, about 10 minutes.
- Bring chicken soup to a simmer in a saucepan over medium-low heat; stir gelatin mixture into soup, dissolving completely. Remove from heat and cool until slightly warm. Stir cream cheese and mayonnaise into soup mixture until smooth; stir Worcestershire sauce and hot sauce into soup mixture.

- Pour soup mixture into food processor with crab mixture and process until smooth, about 1 minute. Pour into a 5-cup mold. Chill in refrigerator until set, about 4 hours.

Nutrition Information

- Calories: 184 calories
- Total Fat: 17.1 g
- Cholesterol: 34 mg
- Sodium: 317 mg
- Total Carbohydrate: 2.7 g
- Protein: 5.6 g

63. Stuffed Mushrooms I

"Incredibly easy and taste even better! There are never any left over!"

Serving: 9 | Prep: 20 m | Cook: 20 m | Ready in: 40 m

Ingredients

- 36 fresh mushrooms
- 1 (8 ounce) package cream cheese, softened
- 1 (6 ounce) can crab meat, drained
- 1/2 teaspoon garlic salt

Direction

- Preheat the oven to 350 degrees F (175 degrees C). Lightly grease a baking sheet with non-stick cooking spray.
- Stem the mushrooms. Reserve 1/3 to 1/2 of the stems and mince them.
- Whip the cream cheese until smooth.
- In a small bowl, combine minced mushroom stems and crabmeat. Blend the cream cheese into the stem and clam mixture. Add garlic salt and mix well. Stuff the mushroom caps with the cheese mixture. Arrange the caps on the prepared baking sheet.
- Bake mushrooms at 350 degrees F (175 degrees C) for 20 minutes, or until the mushrooms and crab mixture are hot, and most of the liquid from the mushrooms has collected in the pan.

Nutrition Information

- Calories: 121 calories
- Total Fat: 9.2 g
- Cholesterol: 44 mg
- Sodium: 240 mg
- Total Carbohydrate: 3.1 g
- Protein: 7.9 g

64. Stuffed Mushrooms II

"Mushrooms stuffed with crabmeat. You can substitute chopped dill for the chopped parsley."

Serving: 10 | Prep: 25 m | Cook: 15 m | Ready in: 40 m

Ingredients

- 1 pound large mushrooms
- 1 1/2 tablespoons vegetable oil
- 4 tablespoons butter
- 1/4 cup minced onion
- 1 (6 ounce) can crab meat, drained
- 1/4 cup cream cheese, softened
- 1 egg, lightly beaten
- 2 cups fresh bread crumbs
- 2 tablespoons chopped fresh parsley
- 1/2 teaspoon salt
- 1/4 teaspoon ground black pepper

Direction

- Preheat oven to 350 degrees F (175 degrees C). Lightly grease a cookie sheet.
- Clean mushrooms and remove stems. Chop enough stem to yield one cup. Use a pastry brush to brush the caps with vegetable oil.
- In a skillet, melt 2 tablespoons butter or margarine. Add chopped stems and onion to the hot butter. Sauté the mixture for 4 minutes, remove it from the heat and let cool.

- In a large mixing bowl, combine the mushroom-onion mixture, crabmeat, cream cheese, egg, 1 cup bread crumbs, parsley, salt, and pepper. Spoon the mixture into the mushroom caps. Arrange the caps on the prepared cookie sheet.
- In a small skillet, melt the remaining butter and add the remaining bread crumbs to the melted butter. Once the bread crumbs are coated lightly sprinkle them over the mushroom caps.
- Bake for 15 minutes.

Nutrition Information

- Calories: 200 calories
- Total Fat: 10.7 g
- Cholesterol: 52 mg
- Sodium: 390 mg
- Total Carbohydrate: 17.7 g
- Protein: 8.9 g

65. Thai Crab Rolls

"Moderately spiced crab meat rolled into Thai spring roll sheets before quickly 'pan' deep-fried and dipped into a magical, tangy dipping sauce! Arrange on lettuce leaves with the dip in the center for a stunning presentation."

Serving: 18 | Prep: 20 m | Cook: 10 m | Ready in: 30 m

Ingredients

- 1 pound crabmeat, drained and flaked
- 1 tablespoon mayonnaise
- 1 tablespoon tamarind paste
- 1 bird's eye chile, seeded and minced
- 2 pinches salt
- 1 (12 ounce) package spring roll wrappers
- 1 egg yolk, beaten
- 1 cup vegetable oil for deep-frying
- 1/4 cup rice vinegar
- 1 teaspoon soy sauce
- 1 clove garlic
- 2 tablespoons white sugar
- 15 butter lettuce leaves, rinsed

Direction

- In a medium bowl, mix together the crabmeat, mayonnaise, tamarind paste, chile pepper and salt. Spoon about 2 tablespoons of the mixture onto the center of a spring roll square. Fold one corner up just past the filling, and press to seal. Brush the open section of the roll with egg yolk. This does not just seal the roll, it also crisps it. Fold the two corners on either side of the folded corner towards the center. Roll up the filling tightly towards the remaining point. Seal the point with a little more egg if necessary. Repeat with remaining wrappers.

- Add enough oil to a heavy skillet to cover the rolls about half way. Heat over medium-high heat until oil is sizzling hot. Fry rolls a few at a time for 45 to 50 seconds, until golden. Remove to paper towels to drain.
- To make the dipping sauce, combine the rice vinegar, soy sauce, garlic clove and sugar in the container of a blender or food processor. Process until smooth.
- To serve, line a serving platter with lettuce leaves, and place a small bowl of the dipping sauce in the center. Arrange crab rolls on top of lettuce leaves around the dip.

Nutrition Information

- Calories: 108 calories
- Total Fat: 2.7 g
- Cholesterol: 36 mg
- Sodium: 213 mg
- Total Carbohydrate: 13.1 g
- Protein: 7.4 g

66. The Best Seafood Stuffed Mushrooms

"If you're a stuffed mushroom connoisseur, this is a must try! These practically melt in your mouth and are always a hit when I've served them to family and friends. The filling can also be used to stuff chicken breasts or fish."

Serving: 6 | Prep: 30 m | Cook: 15 m | Ready in: 45 m

Ingredients

- 1 (8 ounce) package softened cream cheese
- 1 egg yolk
- 1 tablespoon Italian bread crumbs
- 1 green onion, chopped
- 1 tablespoon lemon juice
- 1 teaspoon Worcestershire sauce
- 1 teaspoon garlic powder
- 1 pinch salt and ground black pepper to taste
- 1 (6 ounce) can snow crab, drained
- 1 (4 ounce) can small shrimp, drained
- 12 large white mushrooms, stems removed
- 1 cup Italian bread crumbs

Direction

- Preheat oven to 400 degrees F (200 degrees C). Line a baking sheet with aluminum foil.
- Place cream cheese, egg yolk, 1 tablespoon bread crumbs, green onion, lemon juice, Worcestershire sauce, garlic powder, salt, and pepper in the bowl of a mixer. Mix until smooth and evenly blended. Fold in the snow crab and shrimp. Stuff the

mushrooms with this mixture, and press into the remaining bread crumbs to coat. Place onto baking sheet stuffing-side-up once coated.

- Bake in preheated oven until the mushrooms have softened slightly, 12 to 14 minutes. Set oven to Broil, and broil mushrooms for a few minutes until the tops are golden and bubbly.

Nutrition Information

- Calories: 278 calories
- Total Fat: 15.6 g
- Cholesterol: 132 mg
- Sodium: 389 mg
- Total Carbohydrate: 17.5 g
- Protein: 17.4 g

67. Trinidadian Callaloo Soup

"This is made with callaloo leaves in the West Indies, but in Canada we often have to use spinach leaves, which is just as tasty."

Serving: 8 | Prep: 20 m | Cook: 45 m | Ready in: 1 h 5 m

Ingredients

- 2 slices bacon, chopped
- 2 onions, chopped
- 1 green bell pepper, chopped
- 1 stalk celery, chopped
- 1 clove garlic
- 3 cups water, or as needed
- 2 (10 ounce) packages frozen okra, thawed
- 1 (10 ounce) box frozen chopped spinach, thawed
- 1/4 teaspoon hot pepper sauce, or to taste
- salt and ground black pepper to taste
- 2 (6 ounce) cans crab, drained (optional)

Direction

- Heat bacon in a saucepan over medium heat until fat begins to render, about 2 minutes; stir in onions, green bell pepper, celery, and garlic. Cook and stir mixture until onions are translucent, about 5 minutes.
- Pour water into bacon mixture; stir in okra and spinach. Bring soup to a simmer; cook for 30 minutes. Season with hot pepper sauce, salt, and pepper.
- Blend soup until smooth using an immersion blender. Alternatively, pour soup into a blender no more than half full.

Cover and hold lid down; pulse a few times before leaving on to blend. Puree in batches until smooth.

- Return soup to a simmer in saucepan over low heat; stir in crab. Simmer until crab is heated through, about 5 minutes.

Nutrition Information

- Calories: 112 calories
- Total Fat: 1.9 g
- Cholesterol: 40 mg
- Sodium: 234 mg
- Total Carbohydrate: 12.5 g
- Protein: 12.8 g

68. Vonciels Seafood Salad

"This is a cool summertime salad, great for cook-outs, family reunions, or parties. You can also make your own variations, by adding more, less, or different ingredients, seasonings, or seafood. This variation is a favorite of my family."

Serving: 30 | Prep: 30 m | Cook: 17 m | Ready in: 3 h 47 m

Ingredients

- 2 tablespoons olive oil
- 1 large onion, diced
- 1 pound large shrimp, peeled and deveined
- 1 pound scallops, rinsed and patted dry
- 1 (6 ounce) can crabmeat, drained and flaked
- 1 (12 ounce) can water packed tuna, drained and flaked
- salt and pepper to taste
- 1 tablespoon seafood seasoning, such as Old Bay™
- 1 cup mayonnaise, or to taste
- 2 tablespoons yellow mustard
- 1/2 teaspoon garlic powder, or to taste
- 1 teaspoon dried oregano
- 1/2 teaspoon ground turmeric
- 2 tablespoons white sugar
- 1 large green bell pepper, chopped
- 2 stalks celery, chopped
- 5 hard-cooked eggs, chopped
- 1 hard-cooked egg, sliced
- 1/2 teaspoon paprika, as garnish

Direction

- Heat oil over medium heat in a large skillet and add onions, stirring until translucent, about 7 minutes. Add shrimp, scallops, crab meat and tuna. Cook until shrimp are pink and the scallops are opaque, 8 to 10 minutes. Season with salt, pepper, and Old Bay Seasoning. Remove from heat.
- Whisk together the mayonnaise, mustard, garlic powder, oregano, turmeric and sugar in a large bowl. Mix in the bell pepper, celery and chopped eggs.
- Add seafood and toss until evenly combined. Garnish with eggs slices and sprinkle with paprika.
- Cover and refrigerate for 2 to 3 hours or overnight before serving to let flavors blend.

Nutrition Information

- Calories: 132 calories
- Total Fat: 8.4 g
- Cholesterol: 82 mg
- Sodium: 271 mg
- Total Carbohydrate: 2.7 g
- Protein: 11.1 g

69. Warm Crab Dip I

"This has been a family favorite for many years. Serve this dip with crackers. It can be served hot or cold."

Serving: 32 | Prep: 2 m | Cook: 15 m | Ready in: 17 m

Ingredients

- 3 (8 ounce) packages cream cheese, softened
- 3/4 cup mayonnaise
- 1/4 cup white wine
- 2 (6 ounce) cans crab meat, drained
- 1 teaspoon prepared mustard
- 1 pinch seasoning salt
- 1 dash garlic powder
- 1 pinch onion powder
- 1 dash Worcestershire sauce

Direction

- In a double boiler, melt cream cheese with mayonnaise. Stir in white wine. Mix in crab meat, mustard, seasoning salt, garlic powder, onion powder, and Worcestershire sauce. Heat until entire mixture in warm, stirring occasionally. Thin the mixture with more white wine if you would like your dip's consistency to be thinner.

Nutrition Information

- Calories: 123 calories
- Total Fat: 11.5 g

- Cholesterol: 34 mg
- Sodium: 134 mg
- Total Carbohydrate: 0.8 g
- Protein: 3.8 g

70. Warm Crab Parmesan Dip

"This dip is a huge hit with everyone who tries it. It's even better with fresh crabmeat, but canned works fine. I took it to a party and every person wanted the recipe. Serve it with blue corn chips. This one will really wow them."

Serving: 40 | Prep: 10 m | Cook: 45 m | Ready in: 55 m

Ingredients

- 1 (4.5 ounce) can crabmeat, drained
- 1 (8 ounce) package cream cheese, softened
- 1 cup mayonnaise
- 1 1/2 cups grated Parmesan cheese
- 1 cup sour cream
- 4 cloves garlic, peeled and crushed (or to taste)

Direction

- Preheat oven to 350 degrees F (175 degrees C).
- In a small baking dish, mix the crabmeat, cream cheese, mayonnaise, Parmesan cheese, sour cream and garlic.
- Bake uncovered in the preheated oven until bubbly and lightly browned, about 45 minutes.

Nutrition Information

- Calories: 88 calories
- Total Fat: 8.4 g
- Cholesterol: 16 mg
- Sodium: 107 mg
- Total Carbohydrate: 0.8 g

- Protein: 2.5 g

Chapter 2: Canned Salmon Recipes

***

71. Artichoke and Salmon Salad

"This creamy and tangy salad is delicious a dip for crackers or crudites! Great for low-carb diets!"

Serving: 6 | Prep: 10 m | Ready in: 10 m

Ingredients

- 1 (4 ounce) package cream cheese, at room temperature
- 2 tablespoons chopped fresh parsley
- 1/2 lemon, juiced
- 1 teaspoon Greek seasoning (such as Cavender's®)
- 1 (2.6 ounce) pouch skinless, boneless pink salmon
- 1 (14 ounce) can artichoke hearts, drained and chopped

Direction

- Mix cream cheese, parsley, lemon, and Greek seasoning together in a bowl; fold in salmon and artichoke hearts.

Nutrition Information

- Calories: 111 calories
- Total Fat: 7.5 g
- Cholesterol: 26 mg
- Sodium: 422 mg
- Total Carbohydrate: 6 g
- Protein: 5.9 g

72. Asian Salmon Cakes with Creamy Miso and Sake Sauce

"A tasty flavorful appetizer, or great as a meal that uses lots of wonderful Asian flavors! You can also easily substitute for the ingredients and use leftovers too such as corn instead of onions, leftover salmon (BBQ'd, broiled or baked) instead of fresh or canned - and they still turn out great! A plus crowd pleaser!"

Serving: 6 | Prep: 10 m | Cook: 20 m | Ready in: 30 m

Ingredients

- 1 tablespoon vegetable oil
- 1 teaspoon sesame oil
- 2 cloves garlic, chopped
- 1 green onion, chopped
- 1 tablespoon miso paste
- 1 cup heavy cream
- 1/4 cup sake
- 1/4 cup fresh lime juice
- 1 1/2 cups dry bread crumbs
- 1 (7 ounce) can salmon, drained and flaked
- 1/3 cup chopped onion
- 1/4 cup chopped fresh cilantro
- 1 egg
- 1 tablespoon soy sauce
- 1 tablespoon water
- 2 tablespoons vegetable oil

Direction

- Heat the vegetable oil and sesame oil in a large skillet over medium heat. Add the green onion and garlic, and cook until tender. Stir in the miso paste and sake until blended. Bring to a simmer then stir in the cream and lime juice. Return to a simmer and cook until thickened, about 7 minutes. Remove from heat and set aside.
- In a medium bowl, stir together the bread crumbs, salmon, onion, and cilantro. IN a small bowl, whisk together the egg, soy sauce and water using a fork. Stir about half of this into the salmon mixture, and if it seems dry, stir in a little more until the salmon mixture will stick together in patties.
- Heat the oil in a large skillet over medium-high heat. Form the salmon mixture into 2 inch patties for appetizers, or 4 inch patties for a main dish. Fry patties for about 4 minutes per side, or until golden brown. Serve with the sauce drizzled over, or separately for dipping.

Nutrition Information

- Calories: 406 calories
- Total Fat: 27.1 g
- Cholesterol: 100 mg
- Sodium: 602 mg
- Total Carbohydrate: 24.4 g
- Protein: 13.9 g

73. Asian Salmon Salad

"This easy and flavourful salad is perfect for a hearty lunch or a light dinner."

Serving: 4 | Prep: 15 m | Cook: 15 m | Ready in: 30 m

Ingredients

- 1/4 cup Heinz Tomato Ketchup
- 3 tablespoons teriyaki sauce
- 2 tablespoons lime juice
- 2 tablespoons sesame oil
- 2 tablespoons brown sugar
- 8 cups lightly packed mesclun salad greens
- 2 (7.5 ounce) cans canned salmon, skin and bones removed
- 1 cup thinly sliced carrot
- 1 cup thinly sliced cucumber
- 1/4 cup sliced radish
- 1/4 cup lightly packed cilantro leaves
- 1 teaspoon toasted sesame seeds

Direction

- Stir the ketchup with teriyaki sauce, lime juice, sesame oil and brown sugar until well blended. Reserve.
- Place the salad greens in a large bowl. Separate the salmon into large chunks. Add salmon to the bowl along with the carrot, cucumber, coriander leaves and radish. Toss gently with enough dressing to coat the ingredients. Add more dressing to taste. Sprinkle with sesame seeds just before serving.

Nutrition Information

- Calories: 340 calories
- Total Fat: 15.4 g
- Cholesterol: 47 mg
- Sodium: 1099 mg
- Total Carbohydrate: 22.8 g
- Protein: 28.6 g

74. Asian Salmon Wrap

"Moving around a lot, I find that cities often do not share the same restaurants. I lived in Seattle for a few years, and am now in Pensacola, FL. I missed the Samurai Salmon Wrap from World Wrapps. This is my effort for re-creating this taste sensation. It's a wrap with a fabulous Japanese-Asian flavor and a blend of textures to savor."

Serving: 2 | Prep: 30 m | Ready in: 30 m

Ingredients

- 2 green onions, chopped
- 1/3 cup thinly julienned daikon radish
- 1/3 cup chopped cucumber
- 1 tablespoon rice wine vinegar
- 1 tablespoon soy sauce
- 1/4 teaspoon wasabi paste
- 1/8 teaspoon ground ginger
- 2 (12 inch) flour tortillas
- 1 cup cooked white rice
- 2/3 cup canned salmon, drained
- 2 teaspoons sesame seeds

Direction

- Toss together the green onion, daikon radish, and cucumber in a small bowl. In a separate bowl, whisk together the rice wine vinegar, soy sauce, wasabi paste, and ground ginger.
- Lay to two tortillas onto a flat surface. Divide the rice and place in the center of each tortilla. Top each portion of rice with half of the salmon and half of the vegetable mixture. Drizzle half of the soy sauce mixture over each portion of vegetables. Sprinkle

each with 1 teaspoon sesame seeds. Wrap the edges of the tortillas around the filling completely to serve.

Nutrition Information

- Calories: 891 calories
- Total Fat: 18 g
- Cholesterol: 40 mg
- Sodium: 1551 mg
- Total Carbohydrate: 138.5 g
- Protein: 39.3 g

75. Barry Good Salmon Patty

"Every time I do these for my residents they all just love them. Garnish with fresh parsley and lemon slice."

Serving: 15 | Prep: 20 m | Cook: 20 m | Ready in: 40 m

Ingredients

- 4 pounds pink salmon (such as Chicken of the Sea®), drained, flaked and cartilage removed
- 4 large eggs
- 1 1/2 cups panko bread crumbs
- 3/4 cup mayonnaise
- 2 lemons, juiced
- 2 tablespoons ranch dressing mix
- 1 teaspoon salt
- 1 teaspoon ground black pepper
- 1 teaspoon garlic powder
- 1 teaspoon dried dill
- 1 teaspoon seafood seasoning (such as Old Bay®)
- 1/2 cup white cornmeal
- 1/4 cup vegetable oil, or as needed
- 16 lemon slices
- 16 sprigs fresh parsley

Direction

- Mix salmon, eggs, bread crumbs, mayonnaise, lemon juice, ranch dressing mix, salt, pepper, garlic powder, dill, and seafood seasoning in a large bowl; divide into 15 portions and shape into patties. Dust each patty with cornmeal.

- Heat 1 tablespoon oil in a large skillet. Fry a few patties in hot oil, not overcrowding the skillet, until browned, 3 to 4 minutes per side. Repeat until all patties are cooked. Garnish each with a lemon slice and a sprig of parsley.

Nutrition Information

- Calories: 357 calories
- Total Fat: 18.5 g
- Cholesterol: 106 mg
- Sodium: 864 mg
- Total Carbohydrate: 17.7 g
- Protein: 32.6 g

76. **Busy Students Supper**

"Simple rice and salmon dish I thought up on the way home from school today. When I get around to going grocery shopping I will try it with fresh veggies! Not too gourmet, but quick and nutritious."

Serving: 4 | Prep: 20 m | Cook: 20 m | Ready in: 45 m

Ingredients

- 2 cups vegetable broth
- 1 cup Basmati rice
- 1/2 small onion, chopped
- 1 (14.75 ounce) can salmon, drained and flaked
- 1/2 cup frozen mixed vegetables, thawed
- 1 teaspoon lemon pepper
- 1 teaspoon salt-free garlic and herb seasoning blend
- 1 tablespoon olive oil
- 1/4 cup dry bread crumbs for topping
- 1 pinch paprika

Direction

- Rinse the rice. In a saucepan bring the vegetable broth to a boil. Add rice and stir. Reduce heat, cover and simmer for 20 minutes. Preheat oven to 350 degrees F (175 degrees C).
- In a mixing bowl, combine the onion, salmon, mixed vegetables, lemon pepper and herb seasoning. Mix thoroughly. Grease an 11x7 inch baking dish with the olive oil.
- When rice is done, mix it in with the salmon mixture. Mix thoroughly. Press into the prepared baking dish and sprinkle the bread crumbs and paprika on top.

- Cover with foil and bake in a preheated oven for 20 to 30 minutes.

Nutrition Information

- Calories: 426 calories
- Total Fat: 12.3 g
- Cholesterol: 45 mg
- Sodium: 777 mg
- Total Carbohydrate: 48 g
- Protein: 29.9 g

77. CaribbeanStyle Fried Salmon Fritters

"Adapted from fried Caribbean accras, which are made from salted cod. A recipe that my dad used to make on the occasional Sunday. I didn't have salted cod, so I substituted canned sockeye salmon and it turned out awesome."

Serving: 8 | Prep: 20 m | Cook: 35 m | Ready in: 55 m

Ingredients

- 2 cups whole wheat flour
- 1 tablespoon chopped fresh parsley
- 2 teaspoons baking powder
- 1 teaspoon salt
- 1 teaspoon ground thyme
- 1 pinch ground cumin
- 1 medium onion, finely chopped
- 1 jalapeno pepper, finely chopped
- 2 eggs, or as needed
- 2 (14.75 ounce) cans salmon, drained and flaked
- 1 cup water
- vegetable oil for frying

Direction

- Mix flour, parsley, baking powder, salt, thyme, and cumin together in a large bowl. Add chopped onion and jalapeno pepper; mix again. Add eggs and salmon; mash salmon and mix until combined. Add water and stir into a very thick batter.
- Heat 1/4 inch oil in a frying pan just below the medium heat setting. Scoop up 1 tablespoon batter per fritter; drop carefully

155

into the hot oil in batches of 3. Fry until golden brown, 3 to 5 minutes per side. Transfer to a dish lined with paper towels to drain. Repeat with remaining batter for about 16 fritters in total.

Nutrition Information

- Calories: 304 calories
- Total Fat: 10 g
- Cholesterol: 92 mg
- Sodium: 805 mg
- Total Carbohydrate: 23.8 g
- Protein: 30 g

78. ChickenCheeseFish

"Chicken, cheese and fish come together to form a delicious main course."

Serving: 12 | Prep: 30 m | Cook: 1 h 30 m | Ready in: 2 h

Ingredients

- 2 pounds skinless, boneless chicken breast halves
- 4 cups shredded Cheddar cheese
- 1 cup shredded Swiss cheese
- 4 (3 ounce) cans tuna packed in olive oil
- 2 (16 ounce) cans pink salmon, drained
- 2 cups heavy whipping cream
- 4 eggs, beaten
- 2 cups crumbled feta
- 1 cup shredded mozzarella cheese
- 2 cups ricotta cheese
- 1 (8 ounce) package cream cheese, softened
- 2 eggs, beaten
- 3 cups Italian seasoned bread crumbs
- 2 tablespoons butter, cut into small pieces

Direction

- Preheat oven to 350 degrees F (175 degrees C).
- Line the bottom of a large baking dish with the chicken breasts. Scatter Cheddar and Swiss cheese over top. Flake the tuna and salmon and layer evenly over the cheese. Mix whipping cream with the 4 beaten eggs in a bowl; pour over top of the dish.

- Mix the feta, mozzarella and ricotta cheeses in a bowl; spread over the fish. Mix the cream cheese, 2 beaten eggs, and bread crumbs in a bowl; spread evenly over top of the cheese. Evenly arrange small pieces of butter over entire dish. Cover with aluminum foil.
- Bake in preheated oven for 1 1/2 hours, or until heated through and golden brown on top.

Nutrition Information

- Calories: 914 calories
- Total Fat: 59.1 g
- Cholesterol: 332 mg
- Sodium: 1471 mg
- Total Carbohydrate: 24.6 g
- Protein: 69.2 g

79. Easy Salmon Brown Rice Pasta Salad

"This is a unique twist using brown rice pasta instead of ordinary wheat. This brightly colored tasty salad has wild Alaskan salmon, cherry tomatoes, avocado, fresh spinach, and a variety of other veggies. It is so easy to make. Chill in fridge and then serve!!!"

Serving: 8 | Prep: 20 m | Cook: 10 m | Ready in: 50 m

Ingredients

- 16 ounces dried brown rice pasta
- 1 (10 ounce) package frozen peas
- 2 cups packed fresh spinach, chopped
- 1 (14.75 ounce) can salmon, drained and flaked
- 1 (8 ounce) bottle Italian-style salad dressing (such as Annie's Lemon and Chive Dressing®)
- 1/2 cup finely chopped carrots
- 3/4 cup red cherry tomatoes
- 3/4 cup yellow cherry tomatoes
- 1/4 cup chopped fresh cilantro
- 1 ripe avocado, peeled and sliced
- 1 tablespoon lemon juice
- 1/2 jalapeno pepper, finely chopped

Direction

- Fill a large pot with lightly salted water and bring to a rolling boil. Stir in pasta, and return to a boil. Cook pasta uncovered, stirring occasionally, until it has cooked through, but is still firm to the bite, 10 to 12 minutes.

- Drop frozen peas and spinach into boiling pasta during the last minute of cooking. Drain pasta, peas, and spinach in a colander. Return pasta, peas, and spinach to the pot.
- Stir in salmon and salad dressing until well combined.
- Chill in the refrigerator, about 20 minutes.
- Gently stir in carrots, tomatoes, cilantro, avocado, and lemon juice.
- Garnish with jalapenos.

Nutrition Information

- Calories: 456 calories
- Total Fat: 17.6 g
- Cholesterol: 23 mg
- Sodium: 705 mg
- Total Carbohydrate: 56.5 g
- Protein: 19.1 g

80. Easy Salmon Dip

"Easy prep makes this a great recipe for card night."

Serving: 6 | Prep: 10 m | Ready in: 10 m

Ingredients

- 1 (14.75 ounce) can salmon, drained and flaked
- 1 (8 ounce) package cream cheese, softened
- 1/2 cup sour cream
- 2 tablespoons lemon juice
- 1 clove garlic, minced
- 1 teaspoon dried parsley
- 1/4 teaspoon dried dill
- 1/4 teaspoon salt
- 1/8 teaspoon ground black pepper

Direction

- Stir salmon, cream cheese, sour cream lemon juice, garlic, parsley, dill, salt, and black pepper together in a bowl.

Nutrition Information

- Calories: 288 calories
- Total Fat: 22.1 g
- Cholesterol: 80 mg
- Sodium: 466 mg
- Total Carbohydrate: 2.5 g
- Protein: 19.6 g

81. **Easy Salmon Patties**

"My husband loves salmon patties and I am always finding ways to lighten it up to suit my taste. This recipe taste lighter and crispier."

Serving: 4 | Prep: 20 m | Cook: 10 m | Ready in: 30 m

Ingredients

- 1 (15 ounce) can salmon, drained and liquid reserved
- 1/3 cup chopped onion
- 1 egg
- 1/2 cup all-purpose flour, or more as needed
- 1 1/2 teaspoons baking powder
- 2 cups shortening, or more as needed
- 1/4 cup cornmeal, or as needed

Direction

- Mix salmon, onion, and egg together in a bowl; stir in flour. Stir baking powder and 2 tablespoons reserved salmon liquid together in a separate bowl; stir into salmon mixture until mixture holds together when shaped. Add more flour if mixture is too soft. Add more reserved salmon liquid if mixture is too firm. Shape salmon mixture into small patties.
- Heat shortening in a skillet over medium heat.
- Spread cornmeal into a shallow bowl and press patties into cornmeal until evenly coated on both sides.
- Fry patties in the hot shortening until golden brown, about 5 minutes per side. Transfer patties to a paper towel-lined plate using a slotted spoon.

Nutrition Information

- Calories: 378 calories
- Total Fat: 19.5 g
- Cholesterol: 93 mg
- Sodium: 580 mg
- Total Carbohydrate: 20.6 g
- Protein: 28.5 g

82. Easy Salmon Whole Wheat Pasta Salad

"This is a great pasta salad for spring and summer when the weather is great and you don't want to spend it in the kitchen. It's very kid friendly too."

Serving: 6 | Prep: 15 m | Cook: 10 m | Ready in: 55 m

Ingredients

- 1 (13.25 ounce) package dried whole wheat rotini pasta
- 2 (5 ounce) cans skinless, boneless salmon, drained
- 1 cucumber, thinly sliced
- 2 (5.3 ounce) containers Greek yogurt
- 2/3 cup mayonnaise
- 2 teaspoons dried dill weed
- 1 teaspoon onion powder
- 2 Roma tomatoes, thinly sliced

Direction

- Fill a large pot with lightly salted water and bring to a rolling boil. Stir in rotini, and return to a boil. Cook uncovered, stirring occasionally, until rotini has cooked through, but is still firm to the bite, 10 to 12 minutes. Drain and rinse with cold water.
- Transfer pasta to a large bowl.
- Toss salmon and cucumber in with rotini, flaking the salmon as you stir.
- Combine Greek yogurt, mayonnaise, dill, and onion powder in a small bowl.
- Spoon yogurt mixture over rotini and gently combine.

- Chill in the refrigerator for at least 30 minutes.
- Arrange slices of Roma tomatoes on the salad before serving.

Nutrition Information

- Calories: 521 calories
- Total Fat: 28.6 g
- Cholesterol: 41 mg
- Sodium: 348 mg
- Total Carbohydrate: 46.7 g
- Protein: 23 g

83. Grandmas Famous Salmon Cakes

"This is a recipe for my Grandmother's famous salmon cakes. It is a family recipe that has been passed down through generations. Serve with macaroni and cheese or any other type of side dish."

Serving: 4 | Prep: 10 m | Cook: 20 m | Ready in: 30 m

Ingredients

- 1 (14.75 ounce) can salmon, drained and flaked
- 2 eggs, beaten
- 1 small onion, diced
- 1 teaspoon ground black pepper
- 3 tablespoons vegetable oil

Direction

- Pick through the salmon and remove any bones. In a mixing bowl, beat the eggs and add the diced onion, salmon and pepper. Mix thoroughly.
- Shape into 2 ounce patties; about 7 or 8 patties. In a large skillet over medium heat, heat the oil. Fry each patty for 5 minutes on each side or until crispy and golden brown.

Nutrition Information

- Calories: 307 calories
- Total Fat: 20.3 g
- Cholesterol: 138 mg

- Sodium: 407 mg
- Total Carbohydrate: 2.3 g
- Protein: 27.5 g

84. IndianStyle Salmon Fry

"My mother used to make a simplified version of this that got me through my broke years in college. I've become a big fan of Indian food, so I 'Indianed' up this old favorite. You can tone down the heat by removing the seeds from the chili pepper. Serve it with rice."

Serving: 2 | Prep: 20 m | Cook: 10 m | Ready in: 30 m

Ingredients

- 2 tablespoons olive oil
- 3/4 teaspoon cumin seeds
- 1/2 teaspoon brown mustard seeds
- 1 small onion, sliced into thin half-circles
- 1 clove garlic, minced
- 1 tablespoon minced fresh ginger root
- 1 green chile pepper, chopped
- 10 fresh curry leaves, chopped (optional)
- 1 tomato, diced
- 2 (14.75 ounce) cans salmon, drained and bones removed
- 1/4 cup chopped fresh cilantro

Direction

- Heat the olive oil in a skillet over medium heat; place the cumin and mustard seeds in the hot oil and cook until the seeds begin to pop. Cook and stir the onions in the spice mixture until they brown. Mix in the garlic, ginger, chile pepper, and curry leaves; cook and stir until the garlic becomes golden. Add the tomatoes and stir for a few seconds before adding the salmon, using the back of your stirring spoon to break the salmon into small pieces in the pan; cook until the salmon is heated through, 5 to 10 minutes; remove from heat. Garnish with cilantro to serve.

Nutrition Information

- Calories: 765 calories
- Total Fat: 47.1 g
- Cholesterol: 262 mg
- Sodium: 1783 mg
- Total Carbohydrate: 11 g
- Protein: 81.5 g

85. Jims Salmon Patties

"My mom made these salmon patties all year! They were a favorite of all us kids and the neighbors too."

Serving: 6 | Prep: 15 m | Cook: 10 m | Ready in: 55 m

Ingredients

- 1 (14.75 ounce) can salmon, drained and flaked
- 1 (7.5 ounce) can salmon, drained and flaked
- 1 (4 ounce) packet saltine crackers, crushed
- 2 eggs, beaten
- 2 tablespoons mayonnaise
- 1 1/2 teaspoons Worcestershire sauce
- 1 1/2 teaspoons fresh lemon juice
- 1 teaspoon red pepper flakes
- 1 teaspoon dry mustard
- 2 tablespoons vegetable oil, or as needed

Direction

- Mix both amounts of salmon, crushed crackers, eggs, mayonnaise, Worcestershire sauce, lemon juice, red pepper flakes, and dry mustard together in a bowl. Chill in refrigerator to allow flavors to combine, 30 minutes. Form mixture into 6 patties.
- Heat vegetable oil in a skillet over medium heat; fry the salmon patties until golden brown, about 4 minutes per side.

Nutrition Information

- Calories: 336 calories
- Total Fat: 16.1 g
- Cholesterol: 110 mg
- Sodium: 682 mg
- Total Carbohydrate: 17.1 g
- Protein: 28.8 g

86. JLyns Awesome Salmon Casserole

"I improvised this salmon casserole with items I had on hand in my pantry. I've never been big on casseroles (if you've had my mom's cooking, you'd understand why), but they are definitely an easy way to use up items that would otherwise be sitting in the pantry forever. This recipe is simple enough; feel free to add or supplement as you see fit!"

Serving: 6 | Prep: 10 m | Cook: 45 m | Ready in: 55 m

Ingredients

- 1 tablespoon butter, or as needed
- 1 cup elbow macaroni
- 1 (6 ounce) can salmon, drained
- 1 (10.75 ounce) can condensed cream of mushroom soup
- 2/3 cup milk, or to taste
- 1/2 cup grated Parmesan cheese
- 1 teaspoon salt
- 1 teaspoon ground black pepper
- 1/4 cup French-fried onions

Direction

- Preheat the oven to 350 degrees F (175 degrees C). Butter a 9-inch casserole dish.
- Bring a large pot of lightly salted water to a boil. Cook elbow macaroni in the boiling water, stirring occasionally, until tender yet firm to the bite, about 8 minutes. Drain.
- Combine macaroni, salmon, cream of mushroom soup, 1/2 can of milk, Parmesan cheese, salt, and pepper in a casserole dish.

Mix until well blended. Sprinkle French-fried onions on top.
- Bake in the middle rack of the preheated oven until lightly browned on top, about 30 minutes.

Nutrition Information

- Calories: 275 calories
- Total Fat: 14.4 g
- Cholesterol: 26 mg
- Sodium: 1025 mg
- Total Carbohydrate: 22.3 g
- Protein: 13.2 g

87. Large Salmon Patties

"This is a clone of the large salmon patties served at my favorite restaurants. I always ask them to put cheese sauce on mine."

Serving: 5 | Prep: 15 m | Cook: 35 m | Ready in: 50 m

Ingredients

- 2 (14.75 ounce) cans salmon, drained and bones removed
- 1 cup plain bread crumbs
- 1 small onion, finely chopped (optional)
- 4 large eggs, beaten
- 2 tablespoons all-purpose flour
- 2 teaspoons dill weed
- 2 teaspoons dried basil
- 1 teaspoon garlic salt (optional)
- 1 teaspoon onion powder (optional)
- 2 tablespoons shortening (such as Crisco®)

Direction

- Mix salmon, bread crumbs, onion, eggs, flour, dill, basil, garlic salt, and onion powder together in a bowl; form into 5 large patties.
- Preheat oven to 350 degrees F (175 degrees C).
- Melt shortening in a large frying pan over medium-high heat; fry patties until golden brown, 6 to 8 minutes per side. Transfer patties to a baking dish.
- Bake in the preheated oven until patties are cooked through, about 20 more minutes.

Nutrition Information

- Calories: 483 calories
- Total Fat: 22.4 g
- Cholesterol: 221 mg
- Sodium: 1173 mg
- Total Carbohydrate: 20.4 g
- Protein: 47.2 g

88. Mimosa Salad

"A mimosa is a layered salad based on grated egg yolks - this version combines them with salmon. Garnish with fresh thyme, if desired."

Serving: 4 | Prep: 15 m | Cook: 20 m | Ready in: 55 m

Ingredients

- 2 potatoes
- 2 small carrots
- 4 eggs
- 1/2 onion, minced
- 1 (8 ounce) can salmon, drained and flaked
- 1 tablespoon mayonnaise, or as needed

Direction

- Place potatoes and carrots into a large pot and cover with salted water; bring to a boil. Reduce heat to medium-low and simmer until soft but not mushy, 15 to 20 minutes. Drain and grate the potatoes and carrots.
- Place eggs in a saucepan and cover with water. Bring to a boil, remove from heat, and let eggs stand in hot water for 15 minutes. Remove eggs from hot water and cool under cold running water. Peel and halve each egg. Separate egg whites and yolks. Finely grate the egg whites and crumble the egg yolks.
- Place onion in a bowl and cover with boiling water. Place a plate on top and soak to remove some of the bitterness of the onion, about 5 minutes. Drain.

- Remove any bones from salmon, transfer salmon to a bowl, and mash with a fork. Spread an even layer of salmon onto a plate.
- Sprinkle onion in an even layer over salmon; top with a layer grated egg whites. Spread a thin layer of mayonnaise over the egg whites. Sprinkle carrot over egg white layer; top with another layer of mayonnaise.
- Top carrot layer with grated potato and a final thin layer of mayonnaise. Finish with a layer of crumbled egg yolks.

Nutrition Information

- Calories: 288 calories
- Total Fat: 12 g
- Cholesterol: 212 mg
- Sodium: 318 mg
- Total Carbohydrate: 22.8 g
- Protein: 22.1 g

89. Moms Baked Salmon

"Mom's baked salmon. Comfort food at its best!"

Serving: 3 | Prep: 10 m | Cook: 30 m | Ready in: 40 m

Ingredients

- 2 tablespoons margarine, melted
- 2 teaspoons all-purpose flour
- 1 (16 ounce) can canned salmon, skin and bones removed
- 6 saltine crackers, crumbled
- 1/2 cup milk

Direction

- Preheat oven to 375 degrees F (190 degrees C).
- Pour melted margarine into a small glass baking dish. Stir flour into the melted margarine until all the flour is moistened. Flake salmon into the dish; add crackers. Pour milk over the mixture and stir.
- Bake in preheated oven until cooked through, about 30 minutes.

Nutrition Information

- Calories: 363 calories
- Total Fat: 19.5 g
- Cholesterol: 69 mg
- Sodium: 701 mg
- Total Carbohydrate: 7.6 g

- Protein: 37 g

90. Moms Salmon Mousse

"Easy economical salmon loaf that tastes great! Terrific during Lent. Unlike most fish recipes, this tastes even better the next day. Add a simple white sauce with dill for a more elegant presentation."

Serving: 5 | Prep: 15 m | Cook: 50 m | Ready in: 1 h 5 m

Ingredients

- 1 (16 ounce) can salmon, drained and flaked
- 1 cup fresh bread crumbs
- 1 cup grated carrots
- 1 1/2 teaspoons prepared yellow mustard
- 2 eggs, beaten
- 1/2 cup scalded milk
- 2 tablespoons melted butter
- 3 tablespoons lemon juice
- 1 tablespoon chopped fresh parsley
- 3/4 teaspoon salt
- 1 pinch ground black pepper

Direction

- Preheat the oven to 350 degrees F (175 degrees C). Grease one 8x4 inch loaf pan.
- In a medium bowl, mix together the salmon, bread crumbs, carrots, mustard, eggs, milk, butter, lemon juice, parsley, salt and pepper using your hands until evenly blended. Press into the greased loaf pan.
- Bake for 50 minutes in the preheated oven. Cool 5 minutes before serving.

Nutrition Information

- Calories: 262 calories
- Total Fat: 13.9 g
- Cholesterol: 128 mg
- Sodium: 807 mg
- Total Carbohydrate: 8.1 g
- Protein: 25.1 g

91. Oregon Salmon Patties

"Excellent recipe for canned or fresh salmon patties. This recipe is from the Oregon coast."

Serving: 5 | Prep: 10 m | Cook: 15 m | Ready in: 25 m

Ingredients

- 1 (14.75 ounce) can salmon
- 2 tablespoons butter
- 1 medium onion, chopped
- 2/3 cup cracker crumbs
- 2 eggs, beaten
- 1/4 cup chopped fresh parsley
- 1 teaspoon dry mustard
- 3 tablespoons shortening

Direction

- Drain the salmon, reserving 3/4 cup of the liquid. Flake the meat. Melt butter in a large skillet over medium- high heat. Add onion, and cook until tender.
- In a medium bowl, combine the onions with the reserved salmon liquid, 1/3 of the cracker crumbs, eggs, parsley, mustard and salmon. Mix until well blended, then shape into six patties. Coat patties in remaining cracker crumbs.
- Melt shortening in a large skillet over medium heat. Cook patties until browned, then carefully turn and brown on the other side.

Nutrition Information

- Calories: 441 calories
- Total Fat: 29 g
- Cholesterol: 123 mg
- Sodium: 634 mg
- Total Carbohydrate: 20 g
- Protein: 24.2 g

92. Orzo Salad With Salmon Herbs and Yogurt Vinaigrette

"The rice-shaped pasta known as 'orzo' is a favorite for salads. Here, it's topped with a low-fat yogurt dressing that's also delicious on grilled chicken or a green salad."

Serving: 4 | Prep: 25 m | Cook: 16 m | Ready in: 41 m

Ingredients

- 1 cup orzo pasta
- Vinaigrette:
- 1/3 cup plain low-fat yogurt
- 2 tablespoons fresh lemon juice
- 2 tablespoons extra-virgin olive oil
- 1 tablespoon honey
- 1 teaspoon lemon zest
- 1/4 teaspoon coarse salt
- 1/8 teaspoon freshly ground black pepper
- Salad:
- 1 cup halved cherry tomatoes
- 1 cup peeled and diced English cucumber
- 3 3/4 ounces canned salmon, drained and flaked
- 1 tablespoon minced fresh parsley
- 1 1/2 teaspoons minced fresh chives
- 1 1/2 teaspoons minced fresh dill

Direction

- Bring a large pot of lightly salted water to a boil. Cook orzo in the boiling water, stirring occasionally until tender yet firm to the

bite, about 11 minutes. Drain and transfer to a large bowl.
- Whisk yogurt, lemon juice, olive oil, honey, lemon zest, salt, and pepper together in a bowl until vinaigrette is smooth.
- Mix tomatoes, cucumber, salmon, parsley, chives, and dill with the orzo; add vinaigrette and toss until coated.

Nutrition Information

- Calories: 332 calories
- Total Fat: 9.9 g
- Cholesterol: 13 mg
- Sodium: 264 mg
- Total Carbohydrate: 46.7 g
- Protein: 14.7 g

93. Paleoish Salmon Burgers

"Salmon in a burger-form."

Serving: 8 | Prep: 10 m | Cook: 10 m | Ready in: 20 m

Ingredients

- 1 (14 ounce) can salmon, drained and flaked
- 1 cup gluten-free bread crumbs
- 1/2 cup chopped onions
- 2 eggs, beaten
- 3 tablespoons mayonnaise
- 1 tablespoon chopped fresh parsley
- 2 teaspoons lemon juice
- 1/4 teaspoon garlic salt
- 1 tablespoon olive oil, or more as needed

Direction

- Mix salmon, bread crumbs, onions, eggs, mayonnaise, parsley, lemon juice, and garlic salt together in a bowl; form into patties.
- Heat oil in a grill-pan or skillet over medium heat; cook patties until browned, about 5 minutes per side.

Nutrition Information

- Calories: 201 calories
- Total Fat: 12.2 g
- Cholesterol: 70 mg
- Sodium: 290 mg

- Total Carbohydrate: 8.7 g
- Protein: 13.6 g

94. **Robertas Smoked Salmon Dip**

"I got this recipe from a friend and have been requested by others to share it. It's super easy, cheap and delicious. Don't be tempted to add more smoke flavoring. It will ruin the dish. Also, don't be tempted to add garlic or onions. I made these mistakes before. I recommend using very good crackers to serve with."

Serving: 8 | Prep: 15 m | Ready in: 8 h 15 m

Ingredients

- 1 (6 ounce) can salmon, bones and skin removed
- 1/2 cup mayonnaise
- 1/3 cup finely chopped celery
- 1/3 cup bread crumbs (optional)
- 3 tablespoons lemon juice
- 3 tablespoons chopped fresh dill
- 1 tablespoon liquid smoke flavoring
- 1 tablespoon Cajun seasoning (optional)
- 1 lemon, sliced (optional)
- 1 tablespoon chopped fresh parsley, or to taste (optional)

Direction

- Mix salmon, mayonnaise, celery, bread crumbs, lemon juice, dill, liquid smoke, and Cajun seasoning together in a bowl. Form salmon mixture into a mold on a plate and loosely cover with plastic wrap; refrigerate, 8 hours to overnight. Garnish with lemon slices and parsley.

Nutrition Information

- Calories: 175 calories
- Total Fat: 14.5 g
- Cholesterol: 15 mg
- Sodium: 371 mg
- Total Carbohydrate: 6.4 g
- Protein: 6 g

95. Salmon Avocado Salad

"I came up with this recipe as a substitute for bread. It's very easy and fresh in flavor."

Serving: 2 | Prep: 10 m | Ready in: 10 m

Ingredients

- 1/2 avocado, thinly sliced
- 1/4 cucumber, thinly sliced
- 1 dash lemon juice
- sea salt to taste
- 1 pinch dried dill weed, or more to taste
- 1 (7.5 ounce) can salmon, drained and flaked
- 1 teaspoon creamy salad dressing (such as Miracle Whip®)
- 2 teaspoons capers

Direction

- Layer avocado and cucumber on a serving plate; top with lemon juice, salt, and dill.
- Mix salmon and creamy salad dressing together in a bowl; spoon over avocado and cucumber. Sprinkle capers over salmon mixture.

Nutrition Information

- Calories: 273 calories
- Total Fat: 15.9 g
- Cholesterol: 48 mg
- Sodium: 654 mg

- Total Carbohydrate: 6.5 g
- Protein: 26.3 g

96. Salmon Burgers

"Delicious and quick burgers!"

Serving: 4 | Prep: 10 m | Cook: 15 m | Ready in: 25 m

Ingredients

- 1 (14.75 ounce) can salmon, drained and flaked
- 3/4 cup rolled oats
- 1/2 onion, sliced
- 1 egg
- 1/2 lemon, juiced
- 1 tablespoon Dijon mustard
- salt and ground black pepper to taste
- 1 teaspoon vegetable oil

Direction

- Mix salmon, oats, onion, egg, lemon juice, mustard, salt, and black pepper in a bowl until evenly combined. Divide and shape mixture into four patties.
- Heat vegetable oil in a large skillet over medium-high heat; pan-fry salmon patties until heated through, about 7 minutes on each side.

Nutrition Information

- Calories: 268 calories
- Total Fat: 10.9 g
- Cholesterol: 92 mg

- Sodium: 484 mg
- Total Carbohydrate: 12.9 g
- Protein: 27.8 g

97. Salmon Cakes I

"A salmon, potato and egg mixture, lightly seasoned and fried to a golden crisp. Flaky and crispy on the outside, moist and tender on the inside. Very Tasty!"

Serving: 8 | Prep: 5 m | Cook: 15 m | Ready in: 20 m

Ingredients

- 5 large potatoes, peeled and halved
- 3 cups water to cover
- 1 (14.75 ounce) can canned salmon
- 1 egg
- salt and pepper to taste
- 1/2 cup all-purpose flour
- 1 quart vegetable oil for frying

Direction

- In a small saucepan, cover peeled potatoes with water. Bring water to a boil and cook until tender, about 15 minutes. Let cool and mash.
- In a large bowl, mix together salmon, egg, potatoes, salt and pepper. Mold the mixture into patties (whatever size you choose). Coat both sides of the patties with flour.
- Heat oil over a medium-high heat in a large skillet. Fry the patties (2 or 3 at a time) on both sides until golden brown. Drain on paper towels before serving.

Nutrition Information

- Calories: 398 calories

- Total Fat: 15.7 g
- Cholesterol: 46 mg
- Sodium: 209 mg
- Total Carbohydrate: 46.3 g
- Protein: 18.3 g

98. Salmon Chowder

"I don't like fish, but I LOVE this soup!"

Serving: 8 | Prep: 15 m | Cook: 30 m | Ready in: 45 m

Ingredients

- 3 tablespoons butter
- 3/4 cup chopped onion
- 1/2 cup chopped celery
- 1 teaspoon garlic powder
- 2 cups diced potatoes
- 2 carrots, diced
- 2 cups chicken broth
- 1 teaspoon salt
- 1 teaspoon ground black pepper
- 1 teaspoon dried dill weed
- 2 (16 ounce) cans salmon
- 1 (12 fluid ounce) can evaporated milk
- 1 (15 ounce) can creamed corn
- 1/2 pound Cheddar cheese, shredded

Direction

- Melt butter in a large pot over medium heat. Sauté onion, celery, and garlic powder until onions are tender. Stir in potatoes, carrots, broth, salt, pepper, and dill. Bring to a boil, and reduce heat. Cover, and simmer 20 minutes.
- Stir in salmon, evaporated milk, corn, and cheese. Cook until heated through.

Nutrition Information

- Calories: 490 calories
- Total Fat: 25.9 g
- Cholesterol: 104 mg
- Sodium: 1140 mg
- Total Carbohydrate: 26.5 g
- Protein: 38.6 g

99. Salmon Croquettes

"Salmon croquettes are delicious and easy to fix. Great for a quick dinner and even cold on salad the next day!"

Serving: 2 | Prep: 10 m | Cook: 10 m | Ready in: 20 m

Ingredients

- 1 (6 ounce) can salmon, drained and flaked
- 1 egg
- 1/4 cup finely chopped celery
- 1/4 cup sliced green onion
- 1 tablespoon chopped fresh dill weed
- 1/2 teaspoon garlic powder
- 1/3 cup wheat germ
- 3 tablespoons olive oil

Direction

- In a medium bowl, mix together the salmon, egg, celery, green onion, dill, and garlic powder. Form the mixture into golf ball sized balls, and roll in wheat germ to coat.
- Heat oil in a large skillet over medium heat. Flatten the balls slightly, and fry for about 10 minutes, turning as needed, until golden brown.

Nutrition Information

- Calories: 435 calories
- Total Fat: 30.9 g
- Cholesterol: 130 mg

- Sodium: 360 mg
- Total Carbohydrate: 12.2 g
- Protein: 27.9 g

100. **Salmon Dip**

"One of my favorite recipes! I have had many ask for this recipe. It is always one of the first things gone when I bring it to a barbeque."

Serving: 16 | Prep: 10 m | Ready in: 10 m

Ingredients

- 1 (8 ounce) package cream cheese, softened
- 1/2 cup sour cream
- 1/4 cup butter, softened
- 2 tablespoons chopped pimento peppers
- 1 tablespoon chopped fresh parsley
- 1 teaspoon grated onion
- 1 (7 ounce) can salmon, drained, bones and skin removed
- 1/4 teaspoon dried dill weed

Direction

- In a medium bowl, combine the cream cheese, sour cream, butter, pimentos, parsley and onion; beat with an electric mixer until smooth. Stir in the salmon and dill. Cover and refrigerate until serving.

Nutrition Information

- Calories: 111 calories
- Total Fat: 10.2 g
- Cholesterol: 32 mg
- Sodium: 110 mg
- Total Carbohydrate: 0.8 g

- Protein: 4.2 g

101. Salmon Loaf

"Salmon, cracker crumbs, milk, egg and butter, baked into a loaf."

Serving: 4 | Prep: 5 m | Cook: 45 m | Ready in: 50 m

Ingredients

- 1 (14.75 ounce) can salmon, undrained
- 1/2 cup crushed saltine crackers
- 1/2 cup milk
- 1 egg, beaten
- salt and pepper to taste
- 2 tablespoons melted butter

Direction

- Preheat oven to 350 degrees F (175 degrees C).
- In a mixing bowl, combine the salmon, cracker crumbs, milk, egg, salt, pepper, and melted butter. Mix thoroughly.
- Press the salmon mixture into a lightly greased 9x5 inch loaf pan.
- Bake in a preheated oven for 45 minutes or until done.

Nutrition Information

- Calories: 293 calories
- Total Fat: 16.1 g
- Cholesterol: 110 mg
- Sodium: 536 mg
- Total Carbohydrate: 7.7 g

- Protein: 27.5 g

102. Salmon Mac and Cheese

"This is a salmon version of a tuna casserole. You can use tuna in this as well. I made this up in college when I needed to make something that would use up stuff I had in the kitchen."

Serving: 8 | Prep: 20 m | Cook: 1 h 10 m | Ready in: 1 h 45 m

Ingredients

- 1 (16 ounce) package elbow macaroni
- 1/4 cup butter, softened
- 1 tablespoon olive oil
- 1 small onion, minced
- 1 (6 ounce) can salmon, drained and flaked
- 1 tablespoon seafood seasoning (such as Old Bay®)
- 1 tablespoon red wine vinegar
- 2 1/2 cups shredded Cheddar cheese
- 2 eggs, beaten
- 2 cups milk
- 1/2 cup vegetable stock
- 1 (14.5 ounce) can peas and carrots, drained
- 1 (8 ounce) can whole kernel corn, drained
- salt and pepper to taste
- 3 slices day-old bread
- 3 tablespoons grated Parmesan cheese

Direction

- Preheat an oven to 350 degrees F (175 degrees C). Lightly grease a 9x13 inch baking dish.

- Fill a large pot with lightly salted water and bring to a rolling boil over high heat. Once the water is boiling, stir in the macaroni, and return to a boil. Cook the pasta uncovered, stirring occasionally, until the pasta has cooked through, but is still firm to the bite, about 8 minutes. Drain well in a colander set in the sink. Transfer to a large bowl. Stir the softened butter into the macaroni.
- Heat the olive oil in a skillet over medium heat; cook the onion in the oil until brown, about 5 minutes. Stir in the salmon and seafood seasoning and cook until warmed through, about 5 minutes more. Remove from heat and pour the red wine vinegar into the skillet and set aside to cool.
- Mix together the Cheddar cheese, eggs, milk, and vegetable stock in a large mixing bowl. Add the salmon mixture, peas and carrots, and corn; mix. Stir in the macaroni. Season with salt and pepper. Spread into the bottom of the prepared baking dish.
- Toast the bread and break into small pieces. Combine the toasted bread and Parmesan cheese in a food processor; blend until chopped into crumbs. Sprinkle over top of the dish.
- Bake in the preheated oven until heated through, about 45 minutes. Allow to cool 15 to 20 minutes before serving.

Nutrition Information

- Calories: 581 calories
- Total Fat: 25.3 g
- Cholesterol: 115 mg
- Sodium: 913 mg
- Total Carbohydrate: 61 g
- Protein: 28.2 g

103. Salmon Pea Wiggle

"This easy recipe is made with canned salmon and peas in a milk gravy. Serve on toast or saltine crackers for a quick tasty meal. Yummy!"

Serving: 6 | Prep: 10 m | Cook: 20 m | Ready in: 30 m

Ingredients

- 3 cups whole milk
- 3 tablespoons all-purpose flour
- 2 (14.75 ounce) cans salmon, drained and flaked
- 1 (15 ounce) can baby peas, drained
- salt and freshly ground black pepper to taste

Direction

- Place milk in a large saucepan over medium heat. Bring just to the boiling point, stirring constantly. Gradually whisk in the flour with a fork, and continue cooking and stirring until slightly thickened. Stir in the peas, and let the mixture heat back up to a simmer while stirring constantly. Mix in the salmon, and season with salt and pepper to taste. Continue cooking and stirring until thick and heated through. Serve over saltine crackers or toast.

Nutrition Information

- Calories: 352 calories
- Total Fat: 14.2 g
- Cholesterol: 73 mg
- Sodium: 741 mg

- Total Carbohydrate: 15 g
- Protein: 38.8 g

104. Salmon Salad

"This is a very quick and tasty great salmon salad that can be eaten as a sandwich on thickly sliced specialty bread (fantastic on foccacia). To serve as a salad, mound mixture on a bed of lettuce, or on an avocado half."

Serving: 4 | Prep: 15 m | Ready in: 15 m

Ingredients

- 2 (6 ounce) cans pink salmon, drained
- 1/2 cup finely sliced green onions
- 1/2 cup finely chopped celery
- 1/4 cup mayonnaise
- 3/4 teaspoon lemon juice
- 3/4 teaspoon dried dill
- 3/4 teaspoon seasoned salt

Direction

- In a bowl, combine salmon, green onions, celery, mayonnaise, and lemon juice. Season with dill and salt. Mix well.

Nutrition Information

- Calories: 248 calories
- Total Fat: 17.2 g
- Cholesterol: 43 mg
- Sodium: 571 mg
- Total Carbohydrate: 2.2 g
- Protein: 20.4 g

105. Salmon Salad Sandwich

"'Tuna' salad sandwich with a twist (salmon)! Substitute to your liking to make it even more flavorful."

Serving: 2 | Prep: 20 m | Cook: 5 m | Ready in: 25 m

Ingredients

- 1 (6 ounce) can pink salmon, drained
- 1/2 cup Greek yogurt
- 1/4 cup chopped celery
- 1 tablespoon Dijon mustard
- 1/2 teaspoon lemon juice
- 1/4 teaspoon garlic powder
- 1/8 teaspoon salt
- 1/8 teaspoon ground black pepper
- 1 pinch paprika, or to taste
- 1 onion, halved, divided
- 4 slices gluten-free bread slices, toasted
- 1/2 avocado, sliced, or to taste
- 1 cup baby spinach leaves

Direction

- Combine salmon, Greek yogurt, celery, mustard, lemon juice, garlic powder, salt, pepper, and paprika in a medium bowl.
- Preheat an outdoor grill for medium heat and lightly oil the grate. Grill 1 onion half until tender and beginning to caramelize, 5 to 7 minutes per side. Remove from grill; slice when cool enough to handle.

- Spread salmon salad over each slice of bread. Top with grilled onions, avocado, and baby spinach.

Nutrition Information

- Calories: 614 calories
- Total Fat: 31.8 g
- Cholesterol: 49 mg
- Sodium: 692 mg
- Total Carbohydrate: 55.5 g
- Protein: 27.2 g

106. Salmon Salad Spread

"This is a good sandwich or cracker spread, much like tuna fish or chicken salad. Yummy!"

Serving: 8 | Prep: 15 m | Cook: 15 m | Ready in: 1 h

Ingredients

- 3 large eggs, or more to taste
- 2 (14.75 ounce) cans pink salmon - drained, flaked, and cartilage removed
- 1/2 cup mayonnaise
- 3 tablespoons mustard
- 1/4 cup sweet pickle relish
- 1/4 cup raisins
- 1/4 cup chopped red onion
- 1 teaspoon celery seed
- salt and ground black pepper to taste

Direction

- Place eggs in a saucepan and cover with water. Bring to a boil, remove from heat, and let eggs stand in hot water for 15 minutes. Remove eggs from hot water, cool under cold running water, and peel.
- Mix salmon, mayonnaise, mustard, relish, raisins, red onion, celery seed, salt, and pepper together in a bowl. Chop eggs, add to salmon mixture, and mix.
- Refrigerate salmon salad until chilled completely, at least 30 minutes.

Nutrition Information

- Calories: 329 calories
- Total Fat: 20.7 g
- Cholesterol: 120 mg
- Sodium: 624 mg
- Total Carbohydrate: 8.3 g
- Protein: 27.1 g

107. Salmon Stew Abalos Style

"While not a traditional Filipino dish, my grandmother added the necessary proportions of canned pink salmon, tomatoes, onion, and loads of garlic to make this dish a Filipino family favorite. Serve alone or on top of rice.

"

Serving: 4 | Prep: 10 m | Cook: 25 m | Ready in: 35 m

Ingredients

- 1 tablespoon olive oil
- 4 cloves garlic, minced
- 1 onion, diced
- 1 tomato, diced
- 1 (14.75 ounce) can pink salmon
- 2 1/2 cups water
- bay leaf (optional)
- salt and ground black pepper to taste
- 1 teaspoon fish sauce (optional)

Direction

- Heat the olive oil in a skillet over medium heat. Stir in the garlic and onion; cook and stir until the onion has softened and turned translucent, about 5 minutes. Stir in the tomato and cook until softened, then add the salmon. Flake the salmon and continue cooking for 3 minutes. Stir in water, bay leaf, salt, pepper, and fish sauce. Bring to a simmer. Cover and cook for 20 minutes.

Nutrition Information

- Calories: 223 calories
- Total Fat: 11 g
- Cholesterol: 45 mg
- Sodium: 466 mg
- Total Carbohydrate: 4.8 g
- Protein: 24.9 g

108. Sensational Salmon Loaf

"This recipe has been in my family for years. Served with creamed peas and boiled new (red) potatoes, it makes a yummy meal even the kids love!"

Serving: 9 | Prep: 15 m | Cook: 45 m | Ready in: 1 h

Ingredients

- 1 (14.75 ounce) can salmon, drained and flaked
- 1 1/2 cups crushed saltine crackers
- 1 egg, slightly beaten
- 1/2 cup diced green bell pepper
- 1/2 cup diced onion
- 1/4 cup milk
- 1/2 teaspoon Worcestershire sauce
- 1 dash hot pepper sauce (optional)
- black pepper to taste

Direction

- Preheat oven to 350 degrees F (175 degrees C). Grease a 9x9-inch baking dish.
- In a large bowl, stir together salmon, crackers, egg, bell pepper, and onion. Mix in milk, Worcestershire sauce, and hot pepper. Season with black pepper. Mix well with your hands, and spread into baking dish.
- Bake in a preheated oven until the top is golden brown and a toothpick inserted into the center comes out clean, about 45 minutes. Cut into squares to serve.

Nutrition Information

- Calories: 143 calories
- Total Fat: 5.4 g
- Cholesterol: 41 mg
- Sodium: 308 mg
- Total Carbohydrate: 10 g
- Protein: 12.9 g

109. Slow Cooker Salmon Chowder

"Yummy salmon chowder made in the slow cooker. Garnish with chopped chives and serve it with some sourdough bread on the side for a scrumptious meal!"

Serving: 4 | Prep: 15 m | Cook: 4 h 10 m | Ready in: 4 h 25 m

Ingredients

- 1 tablespoon butter
- 1 tablespoon coconut oil
- 1 potato, diced
- 2 carrots, diced
- 1 (32 ounce) carton chicken broth
- 1 (14.75 ounce) can salmon, drained
- 1 cup milk
- 1 cup chopped kale
- 1/2 cup chopped onion
- 1/2 cup corn
- 1/2 cup shredded Cheddar cheese
- 1 teaspoon garlic powder
- 1 teaspoon dill
- 1/2 teaspoon cayenne pepper
- 1/2 teaspoon salt
- 1/2 teaspoon ground black pepper

Direction

- Heat butter and coconut oil in a large skillet over medium heat. Add potato and carrots; cook and stir until softened, 10 to 15 minutes.

- Transfer potato and carrots to a slow cooker. Stir in chicken broth, salmon, milk, kale, onion, corn, Cheddar cheese, garlic powder, dill, cayenne pepper, salt, and pepper.
- Cook on Low until flavors combine, about 4 hours.

Nutrition Information

- Calories: 403 calories
- Total Fat: 22.4 g
- Cholesterol: 102 mg
- Sodium: 2041 mg
- Total Carbohydrate: 23.2 g
- Protein: 29.9 g

110. Spicy Salmon Melt

"A variation on a tuna melt I came up with one night with some ingredients on hand. Great for a quick meal. The wasabi mayo adds a great kick! Adjust the amount of spice to your taste."

Serving: 4 | Prep: 10 m | Cook: 5 m | Ready in: 15 m

Ingredients

- 1 (14.75 ounce) can salmon
- 1 tablespoon wasabi paste
- 1 cup mayonnaise
- 3/4 cup chopped sweet pickles
- 1/2 pint grape tomatoes, halved
- 4 French or Italian sandwich rolls, split
- 4 slices provolone cheese

Direction

- Place oven rack in topmost position and preheat oven to broil.
- Drain the canned salmon of all liquid. Mix together the salmon, wasabi, mayonnaise, pickles, and tomatoes. Open the rolls and lay out on a baking sheet. Spoon 1/2 cup of the salmon mixture onto the bottom of each roll. Place one slice of cheese on top of the salmon mixture and broil in the preheated oven until the cheese melts and the top sides of the rolls begins to brown.

Nutrition Information

- Calories: 832 calories
- Total Fat: 60.5 g

- Cholesterol: 86 mg
- Sodium: 1412 mg
- Total Carbohydrate: 36.7 g
- Protein: 36.3 g

Chapter 3: Canned Shrimp Recipes

***

111. Amazing Shrimp Stuffed Mushrooms

"My mom makes these mushrooms every year for the holidays and there are NEVER any leftovers! They are the best stuffed mushrooms I have ever had. I now make them any time I go to a holiday party."

Serving: 10 | Prep: 15 m | Cook: 20 m | Ready in: 3 h 50 m

Ingredients

- 20 large white mushrooms, stems removed
- 1 (4 ounce) can small shrimp, rinsed, drained and broken up
- 1/2 cup chive and onion flavored cream cheese
- 1/2 teaspoon Worcestershire sauce
- 1 pinch garlic powder, or to taste
- 1 dash Louisiana-style hot sauce, or to taste
- 3/4 cup grated Romano cheese

Direction

- Lightly grease a 9x13 inch baking dish. Fill a saucepan with water and simmer the mushroom caps over medium heat for 2 minutes, until the mushrooms begin to soften. Remove the mushrooms with a slotted spoon, drain, and let cool, hollow sides down, on paper towels, for about 15 minutes.
- While mushroom caps are cooling, combine the shrimp, cream cheese, Worcestershire sauce, garlic powder, and hot sauce in a bowl and stir to blend well. Spoon about 2 teaspoons of the shrimp mixture into the cap of each mushroom and place, stuffing side up, in the prepared baking dish. Sprinkle the Romano cheese onto each mushroom. Cover and refrigerate

for at least 3 hours or overnight to blend the flavors and firm up the stuffing.

- Preheat an oven to 400 degrees F (200 degrees C). Uncover the dish and bake the mushrooms in the preheated oven for about 15 minutes, until the cheese is browned and bubbling.

Nutrition Information

- Calories: 103 calories
- Total Fat: 6.8 g
- Cholesterol: 41 mg
- Sodium: 188 mg
- Total Carbohydrate: 2.9 g
- Protein: 7.3 g

112. **Authentic Wonton Soup**

"This wonton soup has been perfected through trial and error. Be sure to use fresh ingredients. Please follow all the steps and you will not be disappointed!"

Serving: 8 | Prep: 45 m | Cook: 3 h 12 m | Ready in: 4 h 7 m

Ingredients

- 1 (2 pound) pork tenderloin, or to taste
- 1/4 cup hoisin sauce, divided
- 1 tablespoon red pepper flakes
- 1 pound lean ground pork
- 1 (4 ounce) can small shrimp, drained and chopped
- 1/4 cup bread crumbs
- 2 tablespoons rice vinegar
- 2 tablespoons dried cilantro
- 1 tablespoon minced fresh ginger
- 1 dash soy sauce
- 6 cups chicken stock
- 2 cups beef stock
- 1 (16 ounce) package wonton wrappers
- 1 cup chopped green onions

Direction

- Rub pork tenderloin with 2 tablespoons hoisin sauce. Season with red pepper flakes.
- Place pork tenderloin in a slow cooker. Cook on High until tender, 3 to 4 hours. Cool until easily handled, about 10 minutes. Chop into small pieces.

- Mix remaining 2 tablespoons hoisin sauce, ground pork, shrimp, bread crumbs, rice vinegar, cilantro, ginger, and soy sauce together in a large bowl.
- Place a 3/4-inch round ball of ground pork filling in the center of each wonton wrapper. Brush edges with water; fold and seal.
- Bring chicken stock and beef stock to a low boil in a large pot. Stir in pork tenderloin. Add wontons; cook until ground pork filling is no longer pink in the center, about 7 minutes. Reduce heat to very low.
- Serve soup garnished with green onions.

Nutrition Information

- Calories: 451 calories
- Total Fat: 13 g
- Cholesterol: 116 mg
- Sodium: 1110 mg
- Total Carbohydrate: 42.1 g
- Protein: 39 g

113. AvocadoShrimp Salad

"Shrimp, avocado, tomato and sweet onions with fresh squeezed lime juice, nice on a hot day"

Serving: 4 | Prep: 25 m | Ready in: 25 m

Ingredients

- 2 avocados - peeled, pitted, and cubed
- 2 tomatoes, diced
- 1 small sweet onion, chopped
- 1 pound cooked salad shrimp
- 1 pinch salt and pepper to taste
- 2 tablespoons lime juice

Direction

- Stir together avocadoes, tomatoes, onion, and shrimp in a large bowl. Season to taste with salt and pepper. Stir in lime juice. Serve cold.

Nutrition Information

- Calories: 319 calories
- Total Fat: 17.1 g
- Cholesterol: 196 mg
- Sodium: 203 mg
- Total Carbohydrate: 14.9 g
- Protein: 29.1 g

114. Awesome Egg Rolls

"They are a little time consuming, but they're definitely worth the effort. You can substitute shredded chicken or pork in this recipe. Serve with hot mustard."

Serving: 8 | Prep: 30 m | Cook: 15 m | Ready in: 45 m

Ingredients

- 6 cups cabbage, shredded
- 1 carrot, shredded
- 1/2 cup fresh bean sprouts
- 1 celery stalk, diced
- 2 tablespoons chopped onion (optional)
- 1 (4 ounce) can shrimp, drained
- 2 tablespoons soy sauce
- 1/8 teaspoon garlic powder
- black pepper to taste
- 1 egg, beaten
- cornstarch
- 20 egg roll wrappers
- vegetable oil for frying

Direction

- In a large bowl, mix together cabbage, carrots, sprouts, celery, and onion. Stir in shrimp, soy sauce, garlic powder, and black pepper.
- Pour beaten egg into a skillet placed over medium heat; cook flat and thin, flipping once, until done. Remove from skillet, cool, and chop finely. Stir egg into cabbage mixture. Sprinkle top with cornstarch, mix, and allow to sit 10 minutes.

- Mix 1 tablespoon cornstarch with 2 tablespoons cold water. Set aside.
- Place 2 or 3 tablespoons of the shrimp mixture into the center of an egg roll skin. Dip a spoon into the water and cornstarch mixture, and moisten all corners but the bottom corner. Fold the egg roll skin from the bottom over the mixture, making a tight tube of the shrimp mixture. Fold corners in from the sides, and press to stick against folded roll. Then roll the rest of the way. Repeat with remaining egg roll wrappers.
- Pour vegetable oil into a deep frying pan to a depth of 3 or 4 inches, and heat oil to 350 degrees F (175 degrees C). Carefully place egg rolls into hot oil, and fry until golden brown. Remove to paper towels.

Nutrition Information

- Calories: 208 calories
- Total Fat: 12.3 g
- Cholesterol: 49 mg
- Sodium: 396 mg
- Total Carbohydrate: 17.7 g
- Protein: 7.2 g

115. Brians Easy Stuffed Flounder

"Easy to make and bake stuffed whole flounder. This tastes great and looks beautiful."

Serving: 6 | Prep: 25 m | Cook: 30 m | Ready in: 55 m

Ingredients

- 1 whole flounder
- 1 cup butter, divided
- 1/2 cup chopped celery
- 1/2 cup chopped onion
- 3 cups chicken-flavored dry bread stuffing mix
- 1 (6 ounce) can lump crabmeat
- 1 (4 ounce) can small shrimp, liquid reserved
- 1 teaspoon Old Bay Seasoning TM, or to taste
- 1 teaspoon Cajun seasoning (optional)

Direction

- Preheat the oven to 300 degrees F (150 degrees C). Lay the fish down dark side up. Make an incision next to the backbone on both sides, stopping before the head and tail. Slip the knife in between the flesh and backbone and run the knife down the ribs on both sides of the backbone.
- Melt 1/2 cup of butter in a skillet over medium heat. Sauté the onion and celery in the butter until just tender. Place the stuffing mix into a bowl, and stir the onion and celery into it along with the butter in the pan. Mix in the crab and shrimp with their juices, adding a little more liquid, or more stuffing to get a good consistency.

- Melt the remaining butter, and brush some of it onto a cookie sheet. Stuff the stuffing mixture into the pockets of the flounder, and place the stuffed fish on the cookie sheet. Brush the outside of the fish with melted butter, and season with the Old Bay and if desired, Cajun seasoning.
- Bake for about 25 to 30 minutes in the preheated oven, or just until the flounder flakes easily with a fork.

Nutrition Information

- Calories: 820 calories
- Total Fat: 36.2 g
- Cholesterol: 200 mg
- Sodium: 2204 mg
- Total Carbohydrate: 78.3 g
- Protein: 43.1 g

116. Cheesy Shrimp Meltaways

"These little morsels melt in your mouth. The cheese and shrimp topping becomes puffy while baking. Make sure you serve them hot. This recipe can easily be doubled and frozen, so it's perfect for parties."

Serving: 12 | Prep: 15 m | Cook: 10 m | Ready in: 25 m

Ingredients

- 1 (12 ounce) package English muffins
- 1 (4.5 ounce) can small shrimp, drained
- 1/2 cup butter, softened
- 1 (5 ounce) jar processed cheese spread
- 1 1/2 teaspoons mayonnaise
- 1/2 teaspoon garlic powder
- 1/2 teaspoon seasoned salt

Direction

- Preheat oven to 450 degrees F (230 degrees C).
- Split the English muffins in half and set aside.
- In a mixing bowl, combine the shrimp, softened butter, cheese spread, mayonnaise, garlic powder and seasoned salt. Spread the mixture onto the English muffin halves. Slice each half into 6 or 8 triangles. Place the triangles on a cookie sheet. Bake for 10 minutes, until the mixture begins to melt. Serve immediately.

Nutrition Information

- Calories: 185 calories
- Total Fat: 11.4 g

- Cholesterol: 46 mg
- Sodium: 403 mg
- Total Carbohydrate: 14.2 g
- Protein: 6.8 g

117. Crab and Shrimp Pasta Salad

"Imitation crab meat and mini shrimp make for a wonderful pasta salad that everyone loves!"

Serving: 8 | Prep: 20 m | Cook: 15 m | Ready in: 35 m

Ingredients

- 1 (16 ounce) package uncooked tri-colored spiral pasta
- 1/2 cup mayonnaise
- 1/4 cup apple cider vinegar
- 1/4 cup olive oil
- salt and pepper to taste
- 1 (8 ounce) package imitation crabmeat, flaked
- 1 (6.5 ounce) can tiny shrimp, drained
- 1 pint grape tomatoes, halved
- 1 English cucumber, diced
- 1 (4 ounce) can sliced black olives, drained
- 1 red bell pepper, seeded and chopped

Direction

- Bring a large pot of lightly salted water to a boil. Add the pasta, and cook until tender, about 10 minutes. Drain, and rinse under cold water to cool. Transfer to a large bowl, and set aside.
- In a small bowl, mix together the mayonnaise, vinegar, olive oil, salt and pepper. Pour over the pasta and stir to coat. Add the crab, shrimp, tomatoes, cucumber, black olives and bell pepper; mix gently to coat with the dressing. Taste, and adjust seasoning if desired. If the pasta is too dry, mix in more mayonnaise.

Nutrition Information

- Calories: 446 calories
- Total Fat: 20.6 g
- Cholesterol: 39 mg
- Sodium: 471 mg
- Total Carbohydrate: 50.9 g
- Protein: 14.2 g

118. Delicious Shrimp Dip

"This chip/cracker dip is always the first thing to disappear at any party that I take it to. It's equally delicious with shrimp or crab."

Serving: 40 | Prep: 5 m | Ready in: 4 h 5 m

Ingredients

- 1 (8 ounce) container sour cream
- 1 (8 ounce) package cream cheese, softened
- 1 1/2 cups mayonnaise
- 3 tablespoons Worcestershire sauce
- 3 tablespoons dried parsley
- 1 1/2 teaspoons onion salt
- 1 1/2 teaspoons celery salt
- 1 pinch garlic salt
- 1 (4 ounce) can small shrimp, drained

Direction

- In a medium-sized mixing bowl, combine sour cream, cream cheese, mayonnaise, Worcestershire sauce, parsley, onion salt, celery salt and garlic salt. Mix well. Fold in drained shrimp meat. Cover and chill at least 4 hours, to allow flavors to blend.

Nutrition Information

- Calories: 95 calories
- Total Fat: 9.7 g
- Cholesterol: 16 mg
- Sodium: 217 mg

- Total Carbohydrate: 1 g
- Protein: 1.3 g

119. Fresh Spring Rolls

"These little veggie and shrimp filled wraps are a real hit at parties! Serve them with a spicy dipping sauce."

Serving: 20 | Prep: 20 m | Ready in: 20 m

Ingredients

- 1 cup finely shredded cabbage
- 1 (6.5 ounce) can shrimp, rinsed and drained
- 1/3 cup sweet and sour sauce
- 1/3 cup minced celery
- 1/4 cup shredded carrots
- 20 rice wrappers (6.5 inch diameter)

Direction

- In a medium bowl, mix the cabbage, shrimp, sweet and sour sauce, celery and carrots.
- Fill a small bowl with hot water. Dip rice wrappers one at a time into the water. Allow wrappers to soften, then remove from the water and drain. As wrappers are removed from the water, fill each with 2 tablespoons of the cabbage mixture. Roll the wrappers and chill covered until serving.

Nutrition Information

- Calories: 25 calories
- Total Fat: 0.3 g
- Cholesterol: 11 mg
- Sodium: 30 mg

- Total Carbohydrate: 3.9 g
- Protein: 1.8 g

120. Jomamas Big Game Dip

"This dip has never gotten bad reviews. In fact I use it to make a good first impression at most parties. It takes the normal sour cream and salsa dip and kicks it into an awesome dip for all to overeat. This dip for some reason is A LOT better when served with thin wheat crackers rather than tortilla chips or any other option."

Serving: 24 | Prep: 20 m | Ready in: 20 m

Ingredients

- 1/2 cup sour cream
- 1 (8 ounce) package cream cheese, softened
- 1 (12 ounce) jar medium salsa (such as Pace®)
- 1 (4.5 ounce) can small shrimp, drained
- 2 cups shredded Cheddar cheese
- 1 tomato, chopped
- 1 (6 ounce) can pitted black olives, drained and quartered
- 2 green onions, chopped

Direction

- Beat the sour cream and cream cheese together in a bowl with an electric mixer until smooth.
- Spoon the mixture in an even layer across the bottom of an 8x8-inch pan.
- Spread the salsa over the cream cheese mixture in one layer.
- Follow with layers of shrimp and Cheddar cheese.
- Sprinkle top with chopped tomato, black olives, and green onions.
- Refrigerate for 2 hours to chill and blend flavors before serving.

Nutrition Information

- Calories: 101 calories
- Total Fat: 8.3 g
- Cholesterol: 31 mg
- Sodium: 244 mg
- Total Carbohydrate: 2.3 g
- Protein: 4.8 g

121. Moms Seafood Pasta Salad for a Crowd

"My mother has been making this every summer since I was a child. It keeps well in the fridge and is an ideal accompaniment to hamburgers, hotdogs, ribs...anything BBQ."

Serving: 16 | Prep: 15 m | Cook: 10 m | Ready in: 3 h 25 m

Ingredients

- 1 (32 ounce) package dried small pasta shells
- 4 stalks celery, chopped
- 4 green onions, chopped
- 1/2 (16 ounce) bottle French dressing
- 1/2 (16 ounce) bottle thousand island dressing
- 1/2 cup mayonnaise
- 2 (5 ounce) cans water packed tuna, drained and flaked
- 2 (6 ounce) cans tiny shrimp, drained

Direction

- Bring a large pot of lightly salted water to a boil. Add pasta and cook for 8 to 10 minutes or until al dente; drain.
- In a large bowl, toss together cooked pasta, celery and green onions. Mix in French dressing, thousand island dressing and mayonnaise. Fold in tuna and shrimp. Cover and chill in the refrigerator at least 3 hours.

Nutrition Information

- Calories: 452 calories
- Total Fat: 19.9 g
- Cholesterol: 49 mg
- Sodium: 381 mg
- Total Carbohydrate: 49.9 g
- Protein: 17.2 g

122. Seafood Omelets with Creamy Cheese Sauce

"Thin, rich omelets are wrapped around a crab and shrimp filling. A luscious Cheddar cheese sauce is draped overtop."

Serving: 3 | Prep: 30 m | Cook: 25 m | Ready in: 55 m

Ingredients

- Filling:
- 1/4 cup chicken broth
- 1 tablespoon Dijon mustard
- 1/4 cup heavy cream
- 2 tablespoons butter
- 1 (6 ounce) can crab
- 1 (6 ounce) can salad shrimp
- Sauce:
- 1/4 cup heavy cream
- 1 teaspoon Dijon mustard
- 1 cup shredded Cheddar cheese
- 1 dash nutmeg
- Salt and pepper to taste
- Omelets:
- 4 eggs, beaten
- 1/4 cup heavy cream
- Salt and pepper to taste

Direction

- Prepare the filling by stirring Dijon mustard into chicken broth in a saucepan until dissolved. Bring to a simmer over medium-high heat, then add 1/4 cup cream and 2 tablespoons butter. Reduce heat to medium, and simmer until reduced by half, then stir in crab and shrimp; keep warm over low heat.
- Prepare the sauce by warming 1/4 cup cream, and 1 teaspoon mustard over medium heat. Once hot, whisk in the shredded cheese, then season to taste with nutmeg, salt, and pepper. Keep warm over low heat.
- Whisk eggs, 1/4 cup cream, salt, and pepper together until smooth. Heat an 8-inch non-stick skillet over medium heat, and lightly oil with cooking spray. Pour 1/4 cup of the egg mixture into hot pan, and swirl to make a thin, even layer of egg. Cook until firmed, then flip and cook for a few seconds more to firm the other side.
- To prepare omelets, spoon some of the seafood filling into the lower half of each omelet. Roll up into a cylinder. Serve 2 per person bathed with Cheddar sauce.

Nutrition Information

- Calories: 652 calories
- Total Fat: 50.7 g
- Cholesterol: 536 mg
- Sodium: 852 mg
- Total Carbohydrate: 4.8 g
- Protein: 43.5 g

123. Ship Island Shrimp Dip

"A creamy and delicious dip that is very easy to make and is always a hit! It is even better the second day. Serve with potato chips, crackers or fresh vegetables for dipping."

Serving: 12 | Prep: 5 m | Ready in: 8 h 5 m

Ingredients

- 1 (8 ounce) package cream cheese
- 1 (8 ounce) container sour cream
- 1 lemon, juiced
- 1/2 (.7 ounce) package dry Italian-style salad dressing mix
- 1 (4.5 ounce) can shrimp, rinsed and drained

Direction

- In a medium bowl, combine cream cheese and sour cream and blend with an electric mixer on medium speed until blended.
- Add lemon juice and dressing mix; mix well. Add in shrimp and mix.
- Chill dip overnight and serve.

Nutrition Information

- Calories: 122 calories
- Total Fat: 10.7 g
- Cholesterol: 47 mg
- Sodium: 216 mg
- Total Carbohydrate: 2.2 g
- Protein: 4.5 g

124. Shrimp and Dill Deviled Eggs

"Shrimp and dill add a welcome twist to this picnic favorite. One teaspoon of dried dill weed may be substituted for one tablespoon of fresh dill weed."

Serving: 12 | Prep: 40 m | Cook: 10 m | Ready in: 50 m

Ingredients

- 6 eggs
- 1/4 cup mayonnaise
- 1 (4.5 ounce) can shrimp, rinsed and drained
- 2 tablespoons chopped green onions
- 1 tablespoon chopped fresh dill weed
- 1 tablespoon lime juice
- 2 teaspoons prepared Dijon-style mustard
- 1/4 teaspoon hot pepper sauce
- 1 pinch ground black pepper
- fresh dill weed

Direction

- Place eggs in a medium saucepan and cover with cold water. Bring water to a boil and immediately remove from heat. Cover and let eggs stand in hot water for 10 to 12 minutes. Remove from hot water, cool and peel.
- Slice eggs in half lengthwise. Remove yolks. Set aside whites.
- In a medium bowl, mash egg yolks with a fork. Mix together with mayonnaise, shrimp, green onions, fresh dill weed, lime juice, prepared Dijon-style mustard, hot pepper sauce and ground black pepper.

- Spoon approximately 1 tablespoon egg yolk mixture into each egg white. Garnish with fresh dill weed. Chill in the refrigerator until serving.

Nutrition Information

- Calories: 83 calories
- Total Fat: 6.3 g
- Cholesterol: 113 mg
- Sodium: 103 mg
- Total Carbohydrate: 0.9 g
- Protein: 5.7 g

125. Shrimp Appetizer

"This quick and delicious appetizer is perfect for all occasions. Creamy, zesty and filled with tasty little shrimp, it's particularly good served with buttery round crackers."

Serving: 28 | Prep: 10 m | Ready in: 10 m

Ingredients

- 1 (8 ounce) package cream cheese, softened
- 2 teaspoons Worcestershire sauce
- 1 teaspoon hot pepper sauce
- 1 (8 ounce) jar cocktail sauce
- 2 (6 ounce) containers shrimp, rinsed and drained
- 2 chopped green onions
- 1 tomato, chopped
- 1/2 cup shredded mozzarella cheese

Direction

- In a medium bowl, mix the cream cheese, Worcestershire sauce and hot pepper sauce. Spread the mixture on a medium serving platter. Top with cocktail sauce, and layer with shrimp. Cover the shrimp with green onions, tomato and mozzarella cheese.

Nutrition Information

- Calories: 56 calories
- Total Fat: 3.4 g
- Cholesterol: 31 mg

- Sodium: 159 mg
- Total Carbohydrate: 2.3 g
- Protein: 4 g

126. Shrimp Cream Cheese Spread

"Crackers, bread sticks and vegetables all become fabulous when dipped in this cream cheese base shrimp spread."

Serving: 32 | Prep: 15 m | Ready in: 1 h 15 m

Ingredients

- 2 (8 ounce) packages cream cheese, softened
- 2 tablespoons fresh lemon juice
- 1 teaspoon hot sauce
- 1 (4 ounce) can small shrimp, drained
- 2 green onions, finely chopped
- 1/2 (12 ounce) jar cocktail sauce

Direction

- In a medium bowl, beat together the cream cheese, lemon juice and hot sauce until well blended and fluffy. Mix in the shrimp and green onions. Form into a mound on a medium serving platter. Cover and chill in the refrigerator 1 hour, or until firm. Top with cocktail sauce before serving.

Nutrition Information

- Calories: 58 calories
- Total Fat: 5 g
- Cholesterol: 21 mg
- Sodium: 115 mg
- Total Carbohydrate: 1.6 g
- Protein: 2 g

127. **Shrimp Delight**

"Shrimp lovers and cheese lovers will wrestle for a chance to dip their crackers into this delicious, easy dip!"

Serving: 24 | Prep: 15 m | Ready in: 1 h 15 m

Ingredients

- 1 (8 ounce) package cream cheese, softened
- 1/2 (12 ounce) jar cocktail sauce
- 2 (4 ounce) cans small shrimp, drained
- 1 cup shredded Cheddar cheese

Direction

- In a 9 inch round serving dish, spread the cream cheese. Top with a layer of cocktail sauce. Arrange shrimp evenly over cocktail sauce. Sprinkle Cheddar cheese over all. Chill in the refrigerator approximately 1 hour before serving.

Nutrition Information

- Calories: 69 calories
- Total Fat: 5.1 g
- Cholesterol: 31 mg
- Sodium: 157 mg
- Total Carbohydrate: 1.8 g
- Protein: 4.1 g

128. Shrimp Dip II

"This is a spicy and creamy dip - good for vegetables."

Serving: 12 | Prep: 5 m | Ready in: 5 m

Ingredients

- 1 (8 ounce) package cream cheese, softened
- 1/2 cup mayonnaise
- 1 tablespoon hot pepper sauce
- 2 teaspoons lemon juice
- 1 teaspoon prepared horseradish
- 1/4 teaspoon Worcestershire sauce
- 1 dash red food coloring
- 1 (6 ounce) can small shrimp, drained

Direction

- Combine cream cheese, mayonnaise, chile sauce, lemon juice, horseradish, Worcestershire sauce, red food coloring, and shrimp in a small bowl. Mix well. Serve immediately, or refrigerate. Do not make more than 24 hours in advance.

Nutrition Information

- Calories: 148 calories
- Total Fat: 14.1 g
- Cholesterol: 48 mg
- Sodium: 164 mg
- Total Carbohydrate: 1.1 g

- Protein: 4.7 g

129. Shrimp Garden Salad

"This is my version of a simple garden salad which I changed by adding a small tin of shrimp."

Serving: 6 | Prep: 15 m | Ready in: 15 m

Ingredients

- 1 head romaine lettuce- rinsed, dried and chopped
- 2 bunches radishes, sliced
- 1 bunch green onions, chopped
- 1 cucumber, cleaned and chopped
- 3 tomatoes, chopped
- 3 stalks celery, chopped
- 1 (4.5 ounce) can small shrimp, drained

Direction

- In a large bowl, combine the Romaine, radishes, green onions, cucumber, tomatoes, celery and shrimp. Toss with favorite salad dressing and serve.

Nutrition Information

- Calories: 73 calories
- Total Fat: 0.9 g
- Cholesterol: 37 mg
- Sodium: 77 mg
- Total Carbohydrate: 10.3 g
- Protein: 7.8 g

130. **Shrimp Spread II**

"This is a wonderful hot shrimp spread for crackers. It's quick and easy, and it goes quickly whenever it's served."

Serving: 15 | Prep: 5 m | Cook: 25 m | Ready in: 30 m

Ingredients

- 1 (8 ounce) package cream cheese, softened
- 2 cups shredded Cheddar cheese
- 2 (4.5 ounce) cans shrimp, rinsed and drained
- 4 tablespoons mayonnaise
- 2 tablespoons minced onion
- 1 teaspoon prepared horseradish
- 1/2 teaspoon dried dill weed
- 1 dash vinegar-based hot pepper sauce
- 1 teaspoon lemon pepper
- 1/2 teaspoon paprika

Direction

- Preheat oven to 350 degrees F (175 degrees C).
- In a medium-size mixing bowl, combine cream cheese, Cheddar cheese, shrimp, mayonnaise, onion, horseradish, dill, and hot pepper sauce. Pour mixture into an 8x8 inch baking dish. Sprinkle with lemon pepper seasoning and paprika.
- Bake at 350 degrees F (175 degrees C) for 25 minutes; or until the mixture is bubbly.

Nutrition Information

- Calories: 161 calories
- Total Fat: 13.5 g
- Cholesterol: 63 mg
- Sodium: 220 mg
- Total Carbohydrate: 1.1 g
- Protein: 8.9 g

131. Shrimpy Dressing

"Perfect for all you shrimp lovers out there, this dip or salad dressing is refreshing and goes great with your favorite cracker or vegetables. If you don't have cider vinegar, you can use pickle juice."

Serving: 8 | Prep: 5 m | Ready in: 2 h 5 m

Ingredients

- 1 cup nonfat sour cream
- 1 pinch salt
- 1/3 cup chili sauce
- 1 tablespoon pickle relish
- 1 teaspoon cider vinegar
- 1 tablespoon minced green onions
- 1 (4.5 ounce) can shrimp, drained and chopped
- 1/2 one lemon, juiced
- 1 pinch ground black pepper

Direction

- In a medium bowl, combine sour cream, salt, chili sauce, relish, cider vinegar, onion, shrimp, lemon juice and ground black pepper. Mix well.
- Adjust seasoning and chill before serving.

Nutrition Information

- Calories: 66 calories
- Total Fat: 0.4 g
- Cholesterol: 33 mg

- Sodium: 242 mg
- Total Carbohydrate: 9.2 g
- Protein: 5.1 g

132. Spaghetti Salad III

"This is a very easy salad to make and you can add almost anything to it. We like adding shrimp but you could use tuna or crab."

Serving: 8 | Prep: 10 m | Cook: 15 m | Ready in: 25 m

Ingredients

- 22 ounces spaghetti
- 1 cup chopped celery
- 1 (4.5 ounce) can small shrimp, drained
- 1 onion, chopped
- 1 cup frozen green peas
- 1 (16 ounce) bottle ranch-style salad dressing

Direction

- Break pasta in half and cook in a pot of boiling salted water until al-dente. Drain and cool under cold water.
- In a large bowl, combine the pasta, celery, seafood, onion and peas. Toss with enough dressing to coat. Refrigerate until chilled and serve.

Nutrition Information

- Calories: 613 calories
- Total Fat: 31.7 g
- Cholesterol: 43 mg
- Sodium: 620 mg
- Total Carbohydrate: 64.6 g
- Protein: 15.8 g

133. Sylvias Shrimp Supper

"This is a simple, quick supper that is ready for serving in less than half an hour. Feel free to substitute crab for shrimp and add any vegetables you have on hand, the result is just as tasty! Serve over hot linguini, garnish with a sprinkling of fresh parsley."

Serving: 4 | Prep: 20 m | Cook: 20 m | Ready in: 40 m

Ingredients

- 2 tablespoons butter
- 3/4 cup thinly sliced red onion
- 2 cloves garlic, minced
- 3/4 cup thinly sliced celery
- 1/2 cup thinly sliced carrots
- 4 cups milk
- 1/2 cup all-purpose flour
- 1 bunch fresh parsley, chopped
- 3 tablespoons chopped fresh oregano
- 2 (4 ounce) cans small shrimp, drained
- salt and pepper to taste

Direction

- In a large saucepan melt margarine over medium heat. Add onion, garlic, celery, and carrot. Stir and cook over medium heat until onion is slightly translucent (carrot and celery will remain crunchy).
- Stir in milk and bring mixture to a gentle boil.
- Remove one cup milk from the mixture. Stir flour into the one cup of milk, continue stirring until the flour has dissolved and

there are no lumps. Return the milk and flour mixture to the saucepan. Stir in the parsley, oregano, and salt and pepper to taste. Cook until mixture thickens. Stir in the shrimp and heat through.

Nutrition Information

- Calories: 326 calories
- Total Fat: 12.1 g
- Cholesterol: 132 mg
- Sodium: 274 mg
- Total Carbohydrate: 29.9 g
- Protein: 23.8 g

134. Tangy Catalina Pasta Salad

"A tangy change! All of the vegetables you measure to your taste--you can change the vegetables, too."

Serving: 8 | Prep: 15 m | Cook: 10 m | Ready in: 25 m

Ingredients

- 1 (16 ounce) package elbow macaroni
- 1 (5 ounce) can tuna
- 1 (6 ounce) can small shrimp, drained
- 1/4 cup chopped onion
- 1 green bell pepper, chopped
- 3/4 cup chopped celery
- 1 pinch garlic salt
- 4 tablespoons Catalina salad dressing
- 1 1/2 tablespoons sweet pickle relish
- 3 tablespoons mayonnaise

Direction

- Bring a large pot of lightly salted water to a boil. Add pasta and cook for 8 to 10 minutes or until al dente; drain. Run under cold water to chill, drain again.
- Toss together pasta, tuna, shrimp, onions, green pepper, celery, garlic salt, salad dressing, and relish. Add enough mayonnaise to thin out dressing, if desired.

Nutrition Information

- Calories: 331 calories

- Total Fat: 8.3 g
- Cholesterol: 43 mg
- Sodium: 230 mg
- Total Carbohydrate: 46.7 g
- Protein: 16.5 g

135. Tangy Shrimp Dip

"Tangy and tasty - this is sure to be the best tasting dip at any party. Serve with your favorite crackers or tortilla chips.

"

Serving: 24 | Prep: 20 m | Ready in: 1 h 20 m

Ingredients

- 1 (8 ounce) package cream cheese, softened
- 1/2 cup mayonnaise
- 1/4 cup sour cream
- 2 (4.5 ounce) cans small shrimp, drained
- 1 (8 ounce) jar cocktail sauce
- 1 cup shredded mozzarella cheese
- 1/4 cup chopped green onion
- 1/4 cup chopped green bell pepper
- 1 tomato, chopped

Direction

- In a medium bowl, mix together the cream cheese, mayonnaise and sour cream until smooth. Spread into the bottom of a serving dish. Top with layers in the following order: shrimp, cocktail sauce, mozzarella cheese, green onion, green pepper, and tomato. Cover and refrigerate for 1 hour before serving.

Nutrition Information

- Calories: 105 calories

- Total Fat: 8.4 g
- Cholesterol: 35 mg
- Sodium: 216 mg
- Total Carbohydrate: 2.9 g
- Protein: 4.6 g

136. Tomatoes with Seafood Dressing

"Pureed shrimp dressing, served over garden fresh tomatoes makes a delicious light lunch. It is so simple to prepare, you will want to keep a can of shrimp in the cupboard to dress up a repast for unexpected company."

Serving: 4 | Prep: 35 m | Ready in: 35 m

Ingredients

- 1 cup canned shrimp
- 2 hard-cooked eggs, chopped
- 1 1/2 cups finely grated carrots
- 1 tablespoon minced onion
- 1/2 teaspoon salt
- 1/8 teaspoon ground black pepper
- 1/2 cup mayonnaise
- 2 tablespoons lemon juice
- 1/2 teaspoon prepared mustard
- 4 medium tomatoes
- 4 leaves of lettuce

Direction

- Add shrimp, eggs, carrots, onion, salt, and pepper to the bowl of a food processor. Pulse until just combined. Blend mayonnaise with lemon juice and mustard; mix into shrimp mixture with a fork.
- Core tomatoes. Cut into quarters without cutting all the way to the bottom. Place each tomato on a lettuce leaf, and open. Spoon shrimp mixture into the center. Serve

Nutrition Information

- Calories: 319 calories
- Total Fat: 25.5 g
- Cholesterol: 172 mg
- Sodium: 568 mg
- Total Carbohydrate: 11.6 g
- Protein: 12.4 g

137. Very Easy Shrimp Dip

"A very quick and easy (and tasty!) shrimp dip. Serve with a nice assortment of crackers."

Serving: 8 | Prep: 10 m | Ready in: 10 m

Ingredients

- 1 (8 ounce) package cream cheese
- 1 (4 ounce) can small shrimp, drained
- 1/2 (12 ounce) bottle cocktail sauce

Direction

- Spread the cream cheese on the bottom of an 8 inch square serving dish. Layer the shrimp over the cream cheese. Pour the cocktail sauce over the top.

Nutrition Information

- Calories: 134 calories
- Total Fat: 10.2 g
- Cholesterol: 55 mg
- Sodium: 361 mg
- Total Carbohydrate: 5 g
- Protein: 5.7 g

Chapter 4: Canned Tuna Recipes

***

138. **Antipasto**

"This recipe makes a huge amount. I can it and give it away as Christmas gifts. We usually make this as a group project to cut down on prep time and cost. The ingredient amounts may be altered proportionally as needed."

Serving: 56 | Prep: 1 h | Cook: 30 m | Ready in: 9 h 30 m

Ingredients

- 4 cups chopped cauliflower
- 4 cups pearl onions
- 2 cups chopped red bell peppers
- 2 cups chopped green bell peppers
- 2 cups chopped celery
- 2 cucumbers - peeled, seeded and chopped
- 2 cups carrots, chopped
- 2 cups vegetable oil
- 2 cups distilled white vinegar
- 1 (6 ounce) can tomato paste
- 1 tablespoon pickling spice, wrapped in cheesecloth
- 1 cup black olives
- 1 cup pitted green olives
- 4 cups canned mushrooms
- 1 1/2 (5 ounce) cans tuna, drained and flaked

Direction

- In a large bowl with enough lightly salted water to cover, place the cauliflower, pearl onions, red bell peppers, green bell peppers, celery and cucumbers. Soak 8 to 12 hours, or overnight.

- In a small bowl with enough lightly salted water to cover, place the carrots. Soak 8 to 12 hours, or overnight.
- In a large saucepan, place the vegetable oil, vinegar, tomato paste and pickling spice. Bring the mixture to a boil. Drain and rinse the carrots, and place them in the mixture. Boil 10 minutes.
- Drain and rinse the vegetables in the cauliflower mixture. Place them into the saucepan. Cook 10 minutes, or until the cauliflower is tender but crisp.
- Stir black olives, green olives, mushrooms and tuna into the mixture. Remove the mixture from heat. Discard the wrapped pickling spice. While still hot, transfer to sterile containers and refrigerate.

Nutrition Information

- Calories: 101 calories
- Total Fat: 8.5 g
- Cholesterol: 1 mg
- Sodium: 167 mg
- Total Carbohydrate: 5.1 g
- Protein: 1.8 g

139. AppleKraut Tuna Sandwich

"Sweet apples and sauerkraut combined to make a uniquely flavored tuna sandwich. A low calorie, highly filling snack or meal. You may choose to top the tuna mixture with any of your favorite vegetables."

Serving: 2 | Prep: 15 m | Ready in: 15 m

Ingredients

- 1 (5 ounce) can tuna in water, drained
- 1/4 cup sauerkraut
- 1/4 cup finely chopped apple
- 2 tablespoons Dijon mustard
- 1 tablespoon red wine vinegar
- 4 slices whole wheat bread, toasted

Direction

- Mix tuna, sauerkraut, apple, Dijon mustard, and red wine vinegar in a bowl. Serve on toasted wheat bread.

Nutrition Information

- Calories: 243 calories
- Total Fat: 2.5 g
- Cholesterol: 19 mg
- Sodium: 792 mg
- Total Carbohydrate: 30 g
- Protein: 23.6 g

140. Asian Spicy Tuna Salad

"This tuna salad is one of a kind, simple yet super addictive. Fresh ginger and green chile pepper pair up for this taste explosion!"

Serving: 3 | Prep: 15 m | Ready in: 15 m

Ingredients

- 1 (5 ounce) can solid white tuna packed in water, drained
- 1 teaspoon grated fresh ginger root
- 1/2 teaspoon diced green chile pepper
- 3 tablespoons finely chopped onion
- 1/4 teaspoon curry powder (optional)
- 1/4 cup mayonnaise
- 1/2 teaspoon fresh lemon juice

Direction

- With a fork, flake tuna into a small bowl. Mix in ginger, pepper, chopped onion, curry powder, mayonnaise, and lemon juice.

Nutrition Information

- Calories: 186 calories
- Total Fat: 14.9 g
- Cholesterol: 20 mg
- Sodium: 126 mg
- Total Carbohydrate: 1.9 g
- Protein: 11 g

141. Asian Tuna Salad

"It's spicy and super-addictive! Serve with lettuce as lettuce wraps. Great with crackers and pita bread, too."

Serving: 12 | Prep: 20 m | Ready in: 20 m

Ingredients

- 5 (5 ounce) cans chunk light tuna in water, drained and flaked
- 1/2 cup sweetened dried cranberries (such as Craisins®)
- 1/2 cup finely chopped carrot
- 1/4 cup chopped green onions
- 1/4 cup finely chopped cilantro
- 1 tablespoon sesame seeds
- 1 1/2 teaspoons ground ginger
- 1 1/2 teaspoons ground red chile pepper
- 3/4 teaspoon kosher salt
- 1/2 cup light mayonnaise
- 1/4 cup Asian chile paste (such as sambal oelek)
- 2 tablespoons sesame oil
- 1 tablespoon light soy sauce
- 1 tablespoon honey

Direction

- Mix tuna, cranberries, carrot, green onions, cilantro, sesame seeds, ginger, ground chile pepper, and kosher salt together in a large bowl.
- Whisk mayonnaise, chile paste, sesame oil, soy sauce, and honey together in a separate bowl; add to tuna mixture and stir to coat.

Nutrition Information

- Calories: 157 calories
- Total Fat: 7.1 g
- Cholesterol: 19 mg
- Sodium: 306 mg
- Total Carbohydrate: 10.6 g
- Protein: 13.9 g

142. Atomic Tuna Salad

"Broccoli, cauliflower, onion and celery combine with tuna and fat-free mayo for the perfect tuna salad. Best tuna salad you've ever tasted!"

Serving: 4 | Prep: 20 m | Ready in: 20 m

Ingredients

- 2 (5 ounce) cans tuna, drained
- 1/2 head broccoli, finely chopped
- 1/2 head cauliflower, finely chopped
- 1/2 red onion, finely chopped
- 2 stalks celery, finely chopped
- 1 cup fat-free mayonnaise, or to taste
- 4 pita bread rounds

Direction

- In a large bowl, toss together the tuna, broccoli, cauliflower, onion and celery. Stir in mayonnaise until the salad reaches your desired consistency. Serve on pita bread.

Nutrition Information

- Calories: 317 calories
- Total Fat: 1.5 g
- Cholesterol: 19 mg
- Sodium: 824 mg
- Total Carbohydrate: 53.6 g
- Protein: 24.3 g

143. Best Ever Tuna Salad

"Creamy, delicious tuna salad with a surprise ingredient!"

Serving: 8 | Prep: 15 m | Ready in: 15 m

Ingredients

- 2 eggs
- 2 (5 ounce) cans tuna, drained
- 1 (6 ounce) can crabmeat, shredded
- 1/2 cup mayonnaise
- 1 teaspoon sour cream
- 1 teaspoon yellow mustard
- 1/2 teaspoon dried dill weed
- 1/8 teaspoon lemon pepper
- 2 tablespoons dill pickle relish
- 2 tablespoons sweet pickle relish
- 3/4 cup finely chopped onion

Direction

- Place eggs in a saucepan and cover with cold water. Bring water to a boil and immediately remove from heat. Cover and let eggs stand in hot water for 10 to 12 minutes. Remove from hot water, cool, peel and chop finely.
- In a mixing bowl, combine tuna, crabmeat, mayonnaise, sour cream and mustard. Stir in chopped egg, dill weed, lemon pepper, dill and sweet relish and chopped onion. Mix thoroughly.

Nutrition Information

- Calories: 187 calories
- Total Fat: 12.9 g
- Cholesterol: 80 mg
- Sodium: 260 mg
- Total Carbohydrate: 3.5 g
- Protein: 14.3 g

144. **Best Tuna Casserole**

"This is a tuna casserole that even my picky family loves! The potato chips give the casserole a crunchy crust."

Serving: 6 | Prep: 15 m | Cook: 20 m | Ready in: 35 m

Ingredients

- 1 (12 ounce) package egg noodles
- 1/4 cup chopped onion
- 2 cups shredded Cheddar cheese
- 1 cup frozen green peas
- 2 (5 ounce) cans tuna, drained
- 2 (10.75 ounce) cans condensed cream of mushroom soup
- 1/2 (4.5 ounce) can sliced mushrooms
- 1 cup crushed potato chips

Direction

- Bring a large pot of lightly salted water to a boil. Cook pasta in boiling water for 8 to 10 minutes, or until al dente; drain.
- Preheat oven to 425 degrees F (220 degrees C).
- In a large bowl, thoroughly mix noodles, onion, 1 cup cheese, peas, tuna, soup and mushrooms. Transfer to a 9x13 inch baking dish, and top with potato chip crumbs and remaining 1 cup cheese.
- Bake for 15 to 20 minutes in the preheated oven, or until cheese is bubbly.

Nutrition Information

- Calories: 595 calories
- Total Fat: 26.1 g
- Cholesterol: 99 mg
- Sodium: 1061 mg
- Total Carbohydrate: 58.1 g
- Protein: 32.1 g

145. Bow Tie Pasta with Tomato Tuna Sauce

"Kids love this quick and easy meal. They'll never guess that it's full of nutritious ingredients."

Serving: 8 | Prep: 10 m | Cook: 40 m | Ready in: 50 m

Ingredients

- 1 (16 ounce) package farfalle (bow tie) pasta
- 1 tablespoon olive oil
- 1/2 cup whole wheat bread crumbs
- 1 tablespoon salt
- 1/2 teaspoon ground black pepper
- 1 tablespoon lemon zest
- 1 (15 ounce) can canned beans
- 1 (5 ounce) can tuna, drained
- 2 cups tomato sauce
- 3/4 cup grated Parmesan cheese, divided

Direction

- Preheat an oven to 350 degrees F (175 degrees C). Grease a 9x13 inch baking dish.
- Bring a large pot of lightly salted water to a boil over high heat. Stir in the pasta and boil until cooked through, but still firm to the bite, about 12 minutes. Drain well.
- Heat the olive oil in a large skillet. Toast bread crumbs in oil, about 2 minutes. Season with salt and pepper; stir in lemon

zest. Remove seasoned bread crumbs from skillet and drain on paper towels.
- Place the skillet back over medium heat. Add the beans, and mash. Stir in the tuna, tomato sauce, and 1/4 cup of the Parmesan cheese. Reduce heat to a simmer and cook for 10 to 15 minutes.
- Toss sauce with prepared pasta; place in prepared baking dish. Top with the toasted bread crumbs and remaining 1/2 cup Parmesan cheese. Bake in preheated oven until the cheese melts, about 10 minutes.

Nutrition Information

- Calories: 345 calories
- Total Fat: 5.9 g
- Cholesterol: 11 mg
- Sodium: 1472 mg
- Total Carbohydrate: 56.1 g
- Protein: 18.7 g

146. Campbells Kitchen Tuna Noodle Casserole

"So easy, so delicious, the classic tuna casserole is always a satisfying favorite."

Serving: 4 | Prep: 15 m | Cook: 25 m | Ready in: 40 m

Ingredients

- 1 (10.75 ounce) can Campbell's® Condensed Cream of Mushroom Soup or Campbell's® Condensed 98% Fat Free Cream of Mushroom Soup
- 1/2 cup milk
- 2 tablespoons chopped pimentos (optional)
- 1 cup frozen peas
- 2 (6 ounce) cans tuna, drained and flaked
- 2 cups hot cooked medium egg noodles
- 2 tablespoons dry bread crumbs
- 1 tablespoon butter or margarine

Direction

- Mix soup, milk, pimiento, peas, tuna and noodles in 1 1/2-quart casserole. Bake at 400 degrees F for 20 minutes or until hot. Stir.
- Mix bread crumbs with butter and sprinkle on top. Bake 5 minutes.

147. Campbells Tuna Noodle Casserole

"Campbell's® Condensed Cream of Mushroom Soup flavors a creamy sauce that is mixed with tuna, egg noodles and peas, topped with a crunchy bread crumb topping and baked to perfection."

Serving: 8 | Prep: 10 m | Cook: 35 m | Ready in: 45 m

Ingredients

- 2 (10.75 ounce) cans Campbell's® Condensed Cream of Mushroom Soup (regular or 25% Lower Sodium)
- 1 cup milk
- 2 cups frozen peas
- 2 (10 ounce) cans tuna, drained
- 4 cups hot cooked medium egg noodles
- 2 tablespoons dry bread crumbs
- 1 tablespoon butter, melted

Direction

- Stir soup, milk, peas, tuna and noodles in 3-quart casserole.
- Bake at 400 degrees F for 30 minutes or until hot. Stir.
- Mix bread crumbs with butter in bowl and sprinkle over tuna mixture. Bake for 5 minutes more.

148. Carons Kickin Quinoa Salad

"An easy way to use that tuna you have sitting around and that weird quinoa stuff you got at the health food store. This is great if you want a tuna salad sandwich but don't or can't have bread, or also if you like sushi because it has a nice wasabi kick and a texture reminiscent of sticky rice. And, it has a good crunch and flavor with chopped celery and onion. Quinoa (KEEN-wa) is a 'grain that's not really a grain' used by the ancient Incas. It is especially good for people with wheat or gluten allergies, and can be doctored up with anything for every meal of the day. Try serving on a salad or lettuce leaves for a complete meal and presentation."

Serving: 2 | Prep: 15 m | Cook: 10 m | Ready in: 1 h

Ingredients

- 1/2 cup uncooked quinoa
- 1 cup water
- 1/4 cup chopped celery
- 1/4 cup chopped onion
- 1/4 cup low fat mayonnaise (such as Hellman's® Light)
- 1 teaspoon wasabi powder
- 2 teaspoons lemon juice, or to taste
- salt and ground black pepper to taste
- 1 (5 ounce) can tuna, drained

Direction

- Stir the quinoa and water together in a microwave-safe bowl. Cover; cook in the microwave on High until the water has been absorbed and the quinoa is tender, about 9 minutes. Uncover and place into the refrigerator to cool.
- Place the celery, onion, and mayonnaise together in a bowl. Season with wasabi, lemon juice, salt, and pepper; stir to mix.

Fold in the tuna and chilled quinoa until evenly blended.

Nutrition Information

- Calories: 293 calories
- Total Fat: 5.1 g
- Cholesterol: 19 mg
- Sodium: 410 mg
- Total Carbohydrate: 38.6 g
- Protein: 22.5 g

149. Carries Garlic Pesto Tuna Salad Sandwiches

"I love creating new variations on tuna sandwiches. I made this for my husband's lunch the other day, and he wanted them again for dinner that night! When I made this, I didn't measure anything, just started throwing things in a bowl...adjust to your taste and enjoy!"

Serving: 4 | Prep: 10 m | Ready in: 10 m

Ingredients

- 2 (5 ounce) cans tuna in water, drained
- 2 tablespoons mayonnaise
- 1 tablespoon prepared mustard
- 2 tablespoons basil pesto
- 2 cloves garlic, minced
- 8 slices rye bread
- 8 leaves lettuce
- 1 large ripe tomato, sliced

Direction

- In a medium bowl, mix together tuna, mayonnaise, mustard, pesto, and garlic.
- Make four sandwiches by layering tuna, lettuce, and tomato slices between slices of bread. Serve.

Nutrition Information

- Calories: 342 calories

- Total Fat: 11.9 g
- Cholesterol: 24 mg
- Sodium: 600 mg
- Total Carbohydrate: 34.6 g
- Protein: 23.8 g

150. Cheesy Tuna Dinner

"This quick, one-pan dinner is made with cream of mushroom soup, milk, tuna, green peas and Minute® Rice topped with shredded Cheddar cheese."

Serving: 4 | Prep: 5 m | Cook: 10 m | Ready in: 15 m

Ingredients

- 1 (10.75 ounce) can condensed cream of mushroom soup
- 1 1/2 cups milk
- 2 (6 ounce) cans tuna, drained, flaked
- 1 cup frozen green peas, thawed
- 2 cups Minute® White Rice, uncooked
- 1 cup shredded Cheddar cheese
- French fried onions or crushed potato chips (optional)

Direction

- Mix soup and milk in medium saucepan. Bring to boil on medium heat, stirring frequently.
- Add tuna and peas; mix well. Return to boil.
- Stir in rice and cheese; cover. Reduce heat to low; cook 5 minutes. Stir until cheese is melted. Garnish with canned French fried onions or crushed potato chips just before serving, if desired.

Nutrition Information

- Calories: 936 calories
- Total Fat: 46.6 g
- Cholesterol: 69 mg

- Sodium: 1313 mg
- Total Carbohydrate: 84 g
- Protein: 41.2 g

151. Cheesy Tuna Mornay

"A cheesy Mornay with peas and corn. A great quick dinner that has everything in one dish."

Serving: 6 | Prep: 30 m | Cook: 20 m | Ready in: 50 m

Ingredients

- 1/2 cup uncooked rotini pasta
- 1 tablespoon butter or margarine
- 2 tablespoons all-purpose flour
- 1 1/2 cups milk
- 2 cups shredded Cheddar cheese
- 1 cup frozen green peas
- 1 cup frozen corn kernels
- 2 (7 ounce) cans tuna, drained
- salt
- 1/2 cup bread crumbs

Direction

- Preheat the oven to 350 degrees F (175 degrees C). Bring a pot of lightly salted water to a boil. Add the pasta and cook until tender, about 8 minutes. Drain.
- Meanwhile, melt the butter in a small saucepan over medium heat. Stir in the flour until smooth. Gradually mix in milk so that no lumps form. Stir constantly until the mixture boils, then mix in half of the cheese. Add the peas, corn and macaroni. Drain the tuna, leaving a small amount of liquid to keep it moist. Flake with a fork and stir into the cheese mixture. Transfer to a

casserole dish and top with the remaining cheese. Sprinkle breadcrumbs over the cheese.
- Bake for 20 minutes in the preheated oven, until sauce is bubbly and cheese is browned.

Nutrition Information

- Calories: 423 calories
- Total Fat: 19.8 g
- Cholesterol: 78 mg
- Sodium: 452 mg
- Total Carbohydrate: 26.3 g
- Protein: 34.7 g

152. CinnamonCurry Tuna Salad

"A very simple but delightfully wonderful and versatile tuna salad. Excellent for hors d'oeuvres, it also makes a great sandwich or snack."

Serving: 4 | Prep: 10 m | Ready in: 10 m

Ingredients

- 2 (5 ounce) cans water packed tuna, drained and flaked
- 2 teaspoons mayonnaise
- 1 teaspoon Dijon mustard
- 1 tablespoon sweet pickle relish
- 2 teaspoons lemon juice
- 1 1/2 teaspoons ground cinnamon
- 1 teaspoon curry powder
- 1 teaspoon ground black pepper
- salt to taste

Direction

- In a bowl, mix the tuna, mayonnaise, mustard, relish, lemon juice, cinnamon, curry powder, pepper, and salt. Cover, and refrigerate until ready to serve.

Nutrition Information

- Calories: 101 calories
- Total Fat: 2.5 g
- Cholesterol: 20 mg
- Sodium: 146 mg
- Total Carbohydrate: 3.2 g

- Protein: 16.3 g

153. Clamato Tuna Tostadas

"Chopped fresh veggies are tossed with a seasoned tuna mixture and served on freshly-baked tostadas."

Serving: 10

Ingredients

- 1/2 red onion, sliced
- 2 scallions, chopped
- 1 1/2 tomatoes, chopped
- 2 cucumbers, peeled and chopped
- 2 fresh jalapeno peppers, chopped
- Chopped fresh cilantro
- 4 (6 ounce) cans tuna, drained, flaked
- 6 ounces Clamato® Original
- Fresh lime juice
- Maggi® salsa liquid seasoning
- Worcestershire sauce to taste
- Salt and pepper to taste
- 10 tostada shells

Direction

- Place the red onion into a mixing bowl. Add the chopped scallions, tomatoes, cucumbers, jalapenos and cilantro to the same bowl.
- In a separate serving bowl, combine the tuna, Clamato(R), lime, salsa Maggi(R), Worcestershire sauce, salt and pepper. Mix in the chopped veggies and enjoy over some freshly-baked tostadas.

Nutrition Information

- Calories: 147 calories
- Total Fat: 3 g
- Cholesterol: 20 mg
- Sodium: 166 mg
- Total Carbohydrate: 10.9 g
- Protein: 18.6 g

154. Classic Tuna Noodle Casserole

"Tuna tossed with noodles, peas and pimiento in a creamy sauce is baked until bubbling with crunchy crumb topping."

Serving: 4 | Prep: 10 m | Cook: 25 m | Ready in: 35 m

Ingredients

* 1 (10.75 ounce) can Campbell's® Condensed Cream of Celery Soup or Campbell's® Condensed 98% Fat Free Cream of Celery Soup
* 1/2 cup milk
* 1 cup cooked peas
* 2 tablespoons chopped pimentos (optional)
* 2 (6 ounce) cans tuna, drained and flaked
* 2 cups hot cooked medium egg noodles
* 2 tablespoons dry bread crumbs
* 1 tablespoon butter or margarine, melted

Direction

* Preheat oven to 400 degrees F.
* Mix soup, milk, peas, pimiento, tuna and noodles in 1 1/2-quart baking dish.
* Bake for 20 minutes.
* Mix bread crumbs with butter. Sprinkle on top. Bake 5 minutes or until hot.

155. Cold Macaroni and Tuna Salad

"This is a simple and good recipe that is great served on those hot summer days and can even be prepared the night before so that it is ready and cold when you come home from work the next day. My husband never ate this until we got married and in the summer he requests it every other week. You can substitute chicken for the tuna and it is great that way also. I serve it on a leaf of lettuce, for looks, with an assortment of crackers. Happy eating!"

Serving: 6 | Prep: 25 m | Cook: 18 m | Ready in: 1 h 58 m

Ingredients

- 3 eggs
- 2 3/4 cups macaroni
- 1/2 (10 ounce) package frozen English peas
- 2 (5 ounce) cans tuna, drained
- 3 tablespoons mayonnaise
- 1/4 teaspoon salt
- 1/8 teaspoon ground black pepper

Direction

- Place eggs in a saucepan and cover with water. Bring to a boil, remove from heat, and let eggs stand in hot water for 15 minutes. Remove eggs from hot water, cool under cold running water, and peel.
- Bring a large pot of lightly salted water to a boil. Add macaroni pasta and cook for 8 to 10 minutes or until al dente; drain and rinse under cold water.
- Put frozen peas into a colander and rinse with hot water; drain well.

- Place the macaroni and peas in a large bowl. Dice eggs and add to the bowl. Put the tuna in the bowl, flaking it apart.
- Stir mayonnaise into the mixture a little at a time, so the mixture is moist but not soggy. Sprinkle the salt and pepper and mix one last time. Cover and refrigerate for at least 1 hour or overnight.

Nutrition Information

- Calories: 342 calories
- Total Fat: 9.5 g
- Cholesterol: 108 mg
- Sodium: 220 mg
- Total Carbohydrate: 40.8 g
- Protein: 22.1 g

156. Creamy Tomato Tuna Penne Pasta

"Believe it or not, cream of tomato soup used as a pasta sauce!"

Serving: 2 | Prep: 15 m | Cook: 15 m | Ready in: 30 m

Ingredients

- 6 2/3 ounces tuna packed in olive oil
- 3 cloves garlic, crushed
- 1 teaspoon anchovy paste
- 1 pinch dried oregano
- 1 pinch red pepper flakes, or more as needed
- 3 cups cream of tomato soup, not from concentrate
- 1/2 cup water
- 14 1/2 ounces dry penne pasta
- 2/3 cup finely grated Parmigiano-Reggiano cheese
- 1 tablespoon minced fresh tarragon
- salt and freshly ground black pepper to taste
- 1 pinch red pepper flakes, for garnish
- 1/4 cup finely grated Parmigiano-Reggiano cheese

Direction

- Combine tuna and olive oil, garlic, anchovy paste, oregano, and red pepper flakes in a large saucepan over medium-low heat. Stir and cook for 1 minute once oil begins to sizzle.
- Stir in cream of tomato soup and water. Increase heat to medium and simmer for about 10 minutes.

- Fill a large pot with lightly salted water and bring to a boil. Stir in penne, and return to a boil. Cook pasta uncovered, stirring occasionally, until just slightly undercooked, about 11 minutes; drain.
- Stir cooked pasta into soup mixture; stir in 2/3 cup Parmigiano-Reggiano cheese, and tarragon. Cover and cook for 2 minutes.
- Season with salt and black pepper to taste. Cover and cook for an additional minute.
- Garnish with additional Parmigiano-Reggiano cheese and red pepper flakes.

Nutrition Information

- Calories: 1269 calories
- Total Fat: 22.1 g
- Cholesterol: 62 mg
- Sodium: 3019 mg
- Total Carbohydrate: 202.3 g
- Protein: 72.4 g

157. Creamy Tuna Noodle Casserole From Scratch

"This easy tuna noodle casserole from scratch is made with cream cheese and Gruyere. You can use any small pasta instead of farfalle like penne, rigatoni, etc."

Serving: 4 | Prep: 10 m | Cook: 40 m | Ready in: 50 m

Ingredients

- 1 teaspoon butter
- 12 ounces farfalle (bow tie) pasta
- 9 ounces sour cream
- 1 (8 ounce) package cream cheese, softened
- 1/2 cup milk
- 1 (6 ounce) can chunk tuna in water, drained and flaked
- 1 small green onion, chopped
- 2 tablespoons chopped red bell pepper
- 1 pinch salt and ground black pepper to taste
- 1/2 cup shredded Gruyere cheese

Direction

- Preheat the oven to 375 degrees F (190 degrees C). Grease a baking dish with butter.
- Bring a large pot of lightly salted water to a boil. Cook farfalle pasta at a boil, stirring occasionally, until halfway cooked, about 7 minutes. Drain and rinse under cold water. Drain again.
- Stir together sour cream, cream cheese, and milk in a large bowl until smooth. Mix in tuna, green onion, and red bell pepper. Season with a little salt and pepper. Fold in cooked

farfalle and pour into the prepared baking dish. Sprinkle with Gruyere cheese.
- Bake in the preheated oven until cheese is melted and lightly browned, about 25 minutes.

Nutrition Information

- Calories: 776 calories
- Total Fat: 42.2 g
- Cholesterol: 126 mg
- Sodium: 339 mg
- Total Carbohydrate: 67.2 g
- Protein: 34.1 g

158. Creamy Tuna Pasta Salad

"This tuna salad is extremely fast and delicious. I prepare it with a creamy italian dressing."

Serving: 6 | Prep: 30 m | Ready in: 1 h 30 m

Ingredients

- 1 (8 ounce) package small seashell pasta
- 2 yellow squash, chopped
- 1 zucchini, chopped
- 1/2 cup chopped banana squash
- 1 (15 ounce) can kidney beans, drained and rinsed
- 1/2 (15 ounce) can canned corn
- 2 (5 ounce) cans tuna, drained
- 1/2 cup Italian-style salad dressing

Direction

- Bring a large pot of salted water to a boil. Stir in pasta and return pot to boil. Cook until al dente. Drain well.
- Place squash and zucchini in a medium saucepan with 2 cups of water. Bring to a boil and cook until tender, about 15 minutes. Drain and set aside.
- In a large bowl, combine pasta, squash, zucchini, kidney beans, corn and tuna. Mix well and chill for at least 30 minutes. After salad is chilled, stir in dressing and serve.

Nutrition Information

- Calories: 508 calories

- Total Fat: 8.1 g
- Cholesterol: 13 mg
- Sodium: 440 mg
- Total Carbohydrate: 79.8 g
- Protein: 32.8 g

159. Crispy Rice Bake

"This is a yummy and EASY recipe that kids love! Similar to tuna casserole, but without the noodles. You may add different veggies or use cream of mushroom soup, my family doesn't care for mushrooms, so I use the chicken instead. Can also use fat-free soup."

Serving: 4 | Prep: 5 m | Cook: 45 m | Ready in: 50 m

Ingredients

- 3 cups crispy rice cereal
- 1 cup frozen green peas
- 1 (5 ounce) can tuna, drained
- 1 (10.75 ounce) can condensed cream of chicken soup

Direction

- Preheat the oven to 350 degrees F (175 degrees C). Grease an 8 inch square baking dish.
- In a medium bowl, stir together the tuna, peas and cream of chicken soup. Gently fold in the cereal. Transfer to the prepared baking dish.
- Bake for 45 minutes in the preheated oven, until bubbling and lightly browned on top.

Nutrition Information

- Calories: 211 calories
- Total Fat: 5.1 g
- Cholesterol: 16 mg
- Sodium: 718 mg

- Total Carbohydrate: 28.7 g
- Protein: 13.2 g

160. Crunchy Curry Tuna Sandwich

"An easy tuna sandwich with a crunch and a twist."

Serving: 2 | Prep: 15 m | Ready in: 15 m

Ingredients

- 1 (5 ounce) can tuna, drained
- 1 tablespoon mayonnaise
- 2 tablespoons peanuts
- 2 tablespoons raisins
- 1 stalk celery, finely chopped
- 2 teaspoons curry powder
- salt to taste
- ground black pepper to taste
- 1 pinch white sugar, or to taste
- 1 pinch garlic powder, or to taste
- 1 pinch cayenne pepper, or to taste
- chopped onion (optional)
- chopped green onion (optional)
- 4 slices bread

Direction

- Mix tuna, mayonnaise, peanuts, raisins, and celery in a bowl. Season with curry powder, salt, black pepper, sugar, garlic powder, and cayenne pepper. Stir in onion and green onions. Serve on sliced bread.

Nutrition Information

- Calories: 353 calories
- Total Fat: 12.2 g
- Cholesterol: 22 mg
- Sodium: 576 mg
- Total Carbohydrate: 39.2 g
- Protein: 22.9 g